"**EMS**: It's often life and death. Not everyone can or should do this job; but for those who do, you are on the front lines, and you're the one who answers the calls for help; that's a BIG deal."

- Lance Hodge, Paramedic

THE EMT Book:
An EMT Text and Study Guide

Copyright Lance Hodge, 2018

ISBN-13: 978-1985694736

Printed in the United States of America

Updated: 10-30-21

THE EMT BOOK

An EMT Text and Study Guide

By Lance Hodge, Paramedic

Note: The EMT course I teach is in Los Angeles County, California. Much of what we learn in an EMT course is universal, not varying much from place to place. Some specific information or procedures *will* vary in different states or even counties within a state. Some specific information here may be unique to Los Angeles County, but most is common knowledge needed for all EMT's. You should always defer to *your* most current *local policies and protocols* if they are different from what you find in this text.

Note: Just so you know, when using a period with a parenthesis; if what you're saying can stand alone as a complete sentence the period goes *inside* the parentheses, if it cannot the period goes *outside* the parentheses. I'm editing this book myself, as may soon become obvious, and I've tried to make sure I've followed this and many other grammar rules, but...

Introduction

*Most EMT textbooks are big, fat, **expensive**, and FULL of detailed, and sometimes useless information. I've taught a college EMT course for more than 25 years, and those EMT textbooks, in my opinion, have one main problem; my students didn't read them!*

*This book is different, it's a summary of the 'essential' facts that an EMT must know. It's as short as possible and written so that you'll read it. 'Some' of these facts are BS and won't **ever** matter to you doing your work as an EMT, but they might be questions on some future certification test. Some would argue that the BS I speak of **is** important information so that the EMT "understands" what they are doing and why. In some cases, that's true and that's **not** what I'm talking about. I've included much of that background information if it might improve the student's understanding of the topic. My goal is to leave out most of the crap you don't need and to get straight to the information you **do need**. This book is essentially "notes" derived from my training, and from several of the most current big, fat, expensive EMT textbooks. This is the <u>essential stuff</u> that an EMT should know, straight and to the point.*

●

*<u>**Note**</u>: If you are one of those people that will NOT read a 1,500-page EMT textbook no matter WHAT your instructor tells you, and you intend to learn **everything** from this book, let me give you some advice. Fine, do that. You'll get a TON of other information and training in your EMT course during lectures and lab classes. If you will NOT read that big fat textbook, then use this book to get much of the essential information you'll need. But that big fat textbook has a LOT of other information that is valuable, including photos of injuries and medical conditions and various charts and other information that is either **essential** or **very helpful**. <u>Get that book</u>! At the very least, go through that big fat textbook and look at every single photo and chart and read the description on them.*

About me:

I'm a paramedic. I worked for the *Los Angeles City Fire Department* as a full-time Paramedic until hurting my back carrying a man with congestive heart failure down some stairs.

I handled more than 15,000 9-1-1 calls during my time as a field Paramedic and have dealt with all the things we Paramedics and EMT's deal with. And now, after teaching EMT students for a LONG time I think I can help *you*, as an EMT student, to learn what you *need* to learn.

One thing to remember is that learning involves **study**, and study involves **time**. You'll have to do the sort of studying those "A" and "B" students did in Jr. High and High School. You'll have a TON of things to memorize (learn) and that doesn't come easy or quick.

This book will help, but you'll have to *know* this material, **you'll** have to **study** it, and **memorize** it, so that you'll be able to pass some future tests on this information, and so that you'll know these things that EMT's know in order to best care for the patients you will handle. *The highest level of "patient care" is our goal.*

There's more information, of course, that you'll learn in an EMT class; about the equipment you'll use, and other specific information and local protocols.

You'll have to *practice* assessing patients and using that knowledge and equipment; and that sort of thing can't be covered completely in any book. But this is a BIG part of what you'll need to know, especially to pass that EMT certification test; now read it carefully and learn it!

Lance Hodge

This TV show changed the face of modern EMS

The cast of "Emergency" 1972-1977
Paramedic Roy DeSoto, Dr. Brackett, Nurse Dixie, Dr.Early, Paramedic Johnny Gage

Note: Those in EMS *because* of this TV show are just about gone now, or soon will be. Those old-timers expect you to know about Johnny and Roy and "Emergency" because it was important to 'them' but of course they also think you ought to know the names of the four "Beatles." That show "Emergency" was perhaps THE most important factor in the development of modern EMS and its rapid growth around the country and even the world. History is important. Now go look up the names of the *Beatles*.

mnemonic: (ni-'mä-nik)

Letters that stand for things, used as a memorization aid

Such as A,B,C's for Airway, Breathing, and Circulation

EMS, and this book, is FULL of them!

•

NOTE:

Pages 11-36 are a brief summarized overview of several important topics, to give you a quick and general background in some of the most important aspects of EMT knowledge.

Pages 37-142 summarize hundreds, probably thousands, of miscellaneous items covered in most EMT textbooks.

There are several important diagrams on Pages 143-153.

This is a relatively short book, making it relatively easy to read it twice, or three times, or more, to study this material. You are basically memorizing a TON of new information. You must *know* this material well to pass the EMT tests in your course and then on the National Registry EMT Exam. Study, and *learning*, takes TIME! Devote **significant** study time to this book and to the other information presented in your EMT course!

Contents:

EMT's and Paramedics:

Emergency Medical Technician (EMT) is the basic level of emergency medical training required of most ambulance personnel and of firefighters. The EMT practices *basic life support* (BLS) including CPR, defibrillation with an AED, the use of suction equipment for vomiting or fluids in the airway, the use of oxygen delivery devices, treatment of bleeding, fractures, burns, and various medical conditions. The EMT is also trained in emergency childbirth, the operation of ambulance gurneys, and driving an ambulance or other emergency vehicle.

Paramedics practice *advanced life support* (ALS) including all EMT skills plus the use of a *manual* defibrillator, interpretation of EKG cardiac rhythms, the use of several dozen medications, placement of intravenous lines (IV's) and the use of advanced airways such as endotracheal tubes. Paramedics may also be trained in several advanced procedures such as needle chest decompression, needle cricothyrotomy, and interosseous IV's. **EMT's** are the backbone of EMS, most of the emergencies that occur in EMS systems across the country involve mainly **EMT** level skills.

The History of EMS:

The *Emergency Medical Service (EMS)* in its basic form, began in the late 1960's. More than any other factor it was the 1972 TV show "**Emergency**" that brought about widespread modern EMS. In 1972 when that show premiered, there were only 12 such Paramedic units in the entire country. Ten years later, Paramedics were about 10 minutes away from nearly half of all Americans. Now, nearly fifty years later, our EMS systems still look and sound much like they did on that TV show in 1972; some procedures have changed, but the face of EMS has pretty much remained the same for some fifty years!

The "standard" set by that TV show, and widely adopted across the country, was the *Los Angeles **County** Fire Department* model, with the fire department responsible for emergency medical care. That model is still used today in the *L.A. County Fire Department*; EMT trained firefighters on a firetruck, two firefighter/paramedics on a *Squad* (pickup truck) and a private EMT ambulance company contracted to provide patient transport. The Los Angeles **City** Fire Department model is different, placing their two-person paramedic team in an *ambulance*, with no need for a third resource to provide transport. Some paramedic systems rely on a private company to provide the main EMT *and* paramedic service, while other systems have a "Third Service," with Fire, Police, and EMS all separate departments. In the U.S. it is still most common to use EMT trained firefighters on fire trucks as a primary responder to medical emergencies. Most fire departments *primarily* respond to *medical* emergencies; about 80% of their call volume is *medical*, with only about 20% of their 9-1-1 calls involving fires or other non-medical situations!

Trauma vs. Medical:

Trauma requires some *force* to cause an injury. A **medical** complaint is related to some organ or body system, or medical condition of the patient. A **trauma center** is a specialized and approved hospital that can quickly get patients into life-saving surgery and that have experts and equipment available to treat serious and/or specialized traumatic conditions. Certain hospitals are designated as **heart centers**, **stoke centers** or **pediatric hospitals** to treat those specialized conditions and patients. EMT's should transport their patients to those most appropriate facilities for their specific condition whenever possible. If we take our patient to the *wrong* hospital, it may be very difficult for them to be transferred to the *right* hospital to get the care they need! The transport decisions we make can be the difference between life and death.

CODE 3:

"Code 3" is a common term to describe driving an emergency vehicle with its **red lights and siren** activated, which is deemed necessary when time is critical for saving a life, or to get to the patient quickly for serious emergency treatment, or to get the serious patient quickly to the hospital. When driving Code 3 the vehicle must always be driven with *safety* in mind but may be allowed to exceed the posted speed limit, may be allowed to drive through a red light after stopping first, and may be allowed to cross over double lines in the road or even travel on the 'wrong side' of the road. EMS *(Emergency Medical Service)* personnel must always use *due regard* for public safety when driving Code 3. You are a *professional* driver!

Our transport of patients with a serious complaint should not be delayed. Questioning of the patient can be brief on scene, with additional questions asked in route to the hospital. Paramedics should be called if the patient's complaints are serious, but the EMT is generally allowed to transport such patients without Paramedic intervention if the transport time to the hospital is less than the arrival time of the Paramedics. We can never disregard the rules of the road unless we are going CODE 3, and then only if it is *safe to do so*, and within the guidelines of your employer.

Safety:

EMS personnel need to think *safety first.*

If the scene or patient seems unsafe, we can leave the area, call for police or other backup, and wait until the scene is made safe. We are not supposed to take risks that could endanger our lives! We are not equipped to enter hazardous environments; the fire department has specialized equipment and clothing for that. We are not equipped to handle violent patients or bystanders, the police are trained and equipped for that. Our personal safety is first! The patient must come second.

We should use **personal protective equipment** (PPE) such as gloves, goggles, face masks, and gowns when appropriate. We should have appropriate vaccinations against common communicable diseases.

We do not rush or run into incidents. We should slow down and *size up* (observe) the area for potential dangers. *We* control our actions; we do not let a panicked bystander hurry us into the scene.

A good EMT, a bad EMT:

This job is serious, and important. You will be a member of an elite group that can call themselves an EMT, and that's a big deal.

Much of what we do is not complicated, but a simple mistake, such as laying a patient down that should have been kept sitting, or not laying a patient down who should be, could kill them. We need to study hard, know our job, understand the important *signs* and *symptoms* of injuries and diseases, and be able to quickly do the right thing in any circumstance we encounter.

We answer the calls from 9-1-1, we are the ones who respond on our patient's worst days, and they count on us to know what we're doing and to do it rapidly and correctly. The job of the EMT is an important one, people will trust you with their lives and we must be excellent at what we do.

This job is serious, and important. You will be a member of an elite group that can call themselves an EMT, and that's a big deal.

STUDY:

You are entering a field in which there is a TON of new information to learn. Many people won't pass their EMT course; they won't set aside enough time to study, they won't put in the effort needed to learn all this new material, and they probably aren't *mature enough* to be an EMT.

If the job of an EMT is important to you, perhaps becoming a life-long career, or a stepping stone to some related career, then this is IMPORTANT! Take the time, study hard, be *serious*. An EMT course will require you to study like an "A" or "B" student would study. If you haven't been an A or B student in the past, you need to become one now! This won't be easy, you'll have to work hard, but you can do it, and in a short time you can look back with pride at what you've accomplished. *Take this seriously.*

Along with this book, I advise using an *EMT study app* on your smart phone. Use it frequently, it will help a LOT! For around $5 the "EMT-Tutor" app is excellent, I recommend it; there are several others just as good. My college students are required to spend a *minimum* of **10 minutes a day, _every_ _day_**, working on their *EMT study app*. During our 16-week college class that will equal **18 HOURS of study on that app!** YOU should do that too! *You can pass your EMT course, but it requires a commitment to study hard!*

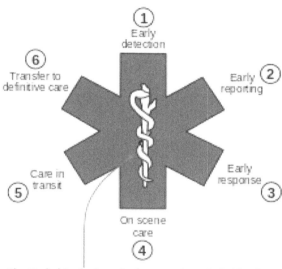

The Rod of Asclepius - Ancient Greek symbol of healing

The Star of Life

The heart: (The cardiac/circulatory system)

The Medical term for the heart muscle is the **myocardium**. <u>Four pumping chambers</u>, the upper are; the **right atrium**, and the **left atrium**. Lower chambers, the **right ventricle**, the **left ventricle**. <u>The left ventricle is the main pumping chamber</u>, it creates an *arterial* pulse with each contraction. (***Arteries*** are the high-pressure vessels, carrying *oxygenated* blood, ***veins*** are low-pressure, and carry ***deoxygenated*** blood.) The *only* exception is *in* the heart, where the *pulmonary artery* carries *deoxygenated* blood out of the right ventricle to the lungs, and the pulmonary *vein* carries ***oxygenated*** blood from the lungs to the left atrium. Confused? YES!

You could remember this diagram by picturing a *"Rat in an RV"* and a *"Lamb in Las Vegas."* Right atrium, tricuspid valve, right ventricle, through the pulmonic valve, into the pulmonary artery, then to the lungs, then through the pulmonary vein, and into the left atrium, mitral valve (also known as the 'bicuspid' valve,) and to the left ventricle.

That's how the blood flows. Deoxygenated blood *gets to* the right atrium from the lower parts of the body through the ***inferior vena cava***, and from the upper parts of the body through the ***superior vena cava***. <u>Inferior</u> (below or lower) and <u>superior</u> (above or higher.) <u>The vena cava are the largest veins in the body.</u> The heart is really <u>two pumps</u>, the right and left side is divided by the *septum*. The blood (from the inferior and superior vena cava) dumps into the right atrium, ***the right heart***, which pumps **out** of the heart and into the lungs. Blood travels through the ***pulmonary artery*** to get to the lungs; by definition, any vessel carrying blood *away* from the heart is called an ***artery***, which is why the *pulmonary artery* carries ***deoxygenated*** blood but is still called an *artery*. That deoxygenated blood gets oxygenated in the lungs, and is pumped back into the left heart, into the left atrium. Since it is

17

blood in a vessel going *back **to*** the heart it is called a ***vein***, even though it now carries ***oxygenated*** blood. *Every* other *artery* in the body carries *oxygenated* blood, and every other *vein* in the body carries *deoxygenated* blood! *The pulmonary artery, and pulmonary vein are the only exceptions to that rule.*

From the *left atrium* it passes through the *mitral valve* (bicuspid valve) then to the *left ventricle* (the main pumping chamber) then through the *aortic valve* and into the ***aorta***. The aorta is the largest artery in the body. The aorta branches out into smaller and smaller *arteries*, then into the smallest arteries called ***arterioles***, and finally into ***capillaries***, which are so small that blood cells may have to go single file through them, and the walls of capillaries are so thin that gasses and nutrients can pass through and get into the surrounding tissues (a ***semi-permeable membrane*** allows gasses and nutrients to pass through them) which is how oxygen and nutrients and wastes gets into and out of cells; then those capillaries take blood back toward the heart, then into tiny veins called ***venules***, then into *veins*, then into the largest veins, the ***vena cava***, and back to the right atrium, and it starts all over again.

A "Heart Attack" is also known as a ***Myocardial Infarction*** or "M.I.". ***Infarction*** means death of tissue. A heart attack may be small or large and is usually preceded by *signs* or *symptoms* such as chest pain, pain radiating to the arm or jaw, nausea, sweating, and dizziness. *(Severe sweating during a heart attack or from some medical condition is called **diaphoresis**.)* If we suspect an M.I., give *low-flow* oxygen with a nasal cannula, at 4-6 liters.

*A "**sign**" is something that can be seen or measured, such as 'skin signs' or 'vital signs.' A "**symptom**" is something the patient complains of that can't be observed or measured, such as dizziness.*

With heart attacks, women often experience additional signs and symptoms different from men, such as sudden shortness or breath, exhaustion, stomach pain, or general upper body pain.

A *heart attack* is usually the result of inadequate blood flow to the heart from blockage within blood vessels *(**Coronary Artery Disease**)* **CAD**, causing pain, and ultimately death (infarction) of some portion of heart tissue. If the area of the damaged heart contains the **pacemaker nodes** *or electrical pathways*, the heart will begin to beat irregularly, and may begin to *fibrillate*.
Fibrillation is a sudden irregular 'quivering' of the heart, which does not pump blood, and results in *cardiac arrest*, and the heart stopping. When the heart stops, breathing stops, and the patient is *clinically* dead. *(**Clinical death** = no heartbeat and no breathing. **Biological death** = lack of brain activity.)* **Cardiac arrest** is also known as **sudden death**, and the patient must be *defibrillated* within the first few minutes to have any chance of survival. EMT's will carry an AED for such situations. An AED is an **Automated External Defibrillator** and is used to deliver a shock to the heart, causing the heart to discharge all its electrical activity, to *stop the fibrillation*, temporarily causing **asystole**, which is a "straight line' on an EKG. Then, if the heart isn't too damaged from the heart attack, the pacemaker cells in the heart will recharge and a functional heartbeat may begin again. This heartbeat is often *irregular*, and fibrillation may occur again. Paramedics have various medications to attempt to stabilize an irregular heartbeat, and to help prevent the heart from going into fibrillation again.

A patient with **Angina**, (*Angina Pectoris* means *chest pain*) has some **coronary artery** or other *heart disease*, and with exertion, or emotional stress, may experience chest pain, from lack of enough oxygen to the heart. Such patients are told to stop and rest and may take *nitroglycerin* pills or spray to treat this condition.
Nitroglycerin *dilates* (expands) *all* arteries, to dilate the **coronary arteries**, to allow more blood to reach the heart muscle. If this condition is not treated quickly the area of the heart deprived of oxygen may suffer an *infarction (death of tissue)*. Nitroglycerin can cause headaches from dilation of arteries in the brain and may cause low blood pressure or shock as arteries dilate and blood pools in the lower extremities. Before taking nitroglycerin the patient should lay down, to avoid the effect of this **vasodilation**. *(Vaso refers to vessels.)*

19

*EMT's can assist a patient with their nitroglycerin. The EMT won't carry such medications on their ambulance, the patient must have them, but EMT's will learn to properly use them. (EMT's can assist with **nitroglycerin**, **albuterol**, and **epinephrine** in an **EpiPen**.)*

The lungs: (The pulmonary system)

The **right lung** has three lobes, the **left lung** has two. The lungs oxygenate the blood. Waste gasses, **carbon dioxide** (CO_2) are expelled from the lungs. Through the nose and mouth air moves into the **trachea**, branches into the right and left **bronchi**, going to each lung. Looking into the mouth we are visualizing the oral → oro? **pharynx**, which ends just a couple of inches beyond the area you can see, at the **epiglottis**, which is right next to the **vocal cords**. The vocal cords are at the entrance to the *trachea*. We can't see the vocal cords or the epiglottis without the use of a **laryngoscope**, which is generally a Paramedic tool. Paramedics can use an **endotracheal tube** or other advanced airway and place that tube between the vocal cords and into the trachea. EMT airways are not that long, and work to keep the tongue from blocking the airway, but do not go beyond the *oral pharynx*. Those EMT airways are the **oropharyngeal** (OPA) or **nasopharyngeal** (NPA) airway.

Complaints of trouble breathing may be **acute** (sudden) or **chronic** (long-term). *Shortness of breath* (SOB) is always taken seriously and requires rapid intervention and rapid transport.

We worry about blockages of the airway, which might be **physical obstructions**, such as food or other items someone might choke on, or **anatomical obstructions**, which might be from an allergic reaction, smoke, or other issues causing swelling. We can use techniques such as the **Heimlich Maneuver** to try to relieve a *physical* obstruction but will need some tool or medication to deal with an *anatomical* obstruction. We will have a **positive pressure** breathing device to try to force air into the airways when needed, often called either a **bag mask device** (BMD) or **bag-valve-mask** (BVM). The EMT will rarely, if ever, do **mouth-to-mouth** breathing on patients, and will instead use our positive pressure breathing devices. *Positive pressure* breathing, *forcing* air in under pressure, is only needed if the patient is not breathing often enough (**respiratory *rate***) or if their breathing is not deep enough (***tidal volume***). A *normal breathing rate* is about **12 times per minute**, or **once every 5 seconds**. We assess *tidal volume* by looking for adequate rise of the chest, the sound or feel of air moving from the nose or mouth, along with an assessment of the patient's skin color. When oxygenation is not adequate, the patient's skin will become bluish (**cyanosis**.) If the patient is not breathing, or if we are not *certain* that breathing is adequate, we will breathe *for* the patient, or *assist* (add to) their inadequate breathing, using our positive pressure breathing device. You will learn and practice the ***head-tilt chin-lift*** to open the airway, pushing down on the forehead and pulling up on the chin, which will move the tongue away from the back of the throat. The tongue is attached to the lower jaw (**mandible**) and moving the jaw upward will move the tongue up, to help open the airway. An open airway is referred to as a ***patent*** airway. With most complaints of **SOB** (shortness of breath) we should give ***high-flow*** oxygen by face mask or assist with a *bag mask device*.

Asthma:

Causes a narrowing of the ***bronchioles***, usually causing ***wheezing***, as the air must move faster through the smaller airways, causing a whistling sound. A ***bronchodilator***, such as an ***albuterol*** inhaler, dilates (opens) the bronchioles, allowing more air to the lungs. *Constriction* of the bronchioles can also occur from things like smoke inhalation, and allergic reactions.

Anaphylaxis:

A ***severe allergic reaction*** is called ***anaphylaxis***, and creates a risk of restricted breathing, and must be treated quickly. An ***anaphylactic reaction*** often causes itching, swelling, and skin rash. An *EpiPen* can treat anaphylaxis, and contains ***epinephrine***, which also has bronchodilation effects. EMT's can assist patients who have medications such as albuterol and epinephrine, to treat respiratory emergencies.

Emphysema:

This is the classic **COPD** disease. *(Chronic Obstructive Pulmonary Disease.)* **Chronic** (long-term) damage to the **alveoli** (air sacs) of the lungs, causing difficulty breathing *(dyspnea.)* Often caused by smoking. The patient often has a large chest *(barrel chest)* from chronic over inflation from strained breathing, may sit in a **tripod position** (arms out supporting themselves, to help inflate their chest) and may have **perioral cyanosis** (blueness around the lips) from the inability to exhale enough CO2. They often speak in short sentences *(one or two-word dyspnea)* since breathing is so difficult. These patients often have oxygen at home, using a **nasal cannula** with a long tube and a large at-home oxygen tank. Their oxygen is most often set at very **low flow**, about 2 liters. Since their alveoli are damaged, they cannot properly absorb oxygen. **High-flow oxygen** by face mask or bag device (10-15 liters) will be needed, if their **chief complaint** is shortness of breath, but can cause **respiratory depression** (breathing rate and tidal volume slows down.) If this occurs, do NOT decrease the oxygen, but use the *bag mask device* to assist their breathing. If the COPD patient has called you for some *other* reason, *not* for trouble breathing, then leave them on their low-flow oxygen during treatment and transport. *(Oxygen flow rates are often determined by the patient's blood levels of oxygen as measured by a **Pulse Oximeter**.)*

Chronic bronchitis:

This is another COPD disease. Enlarged mucus glands will cause congestion and coughing from excess mucus (**sputum**) production. Any patient with trouble breathing should be kept sitting up, and needs high-flow oxygen, and/or assistance with our *bag mask device.*

Congestive Heart Failure (CHF):

Can generally be referred to as simply "**heart failure**." A common form of heart failure is caused by **left-sided** heart problems, leading to a build up of pressure in the lungs where fluid can leak from over pressurized capillaries and begin to fill the lung. This fluid in the lungs causes **rales**, also known as **crackles**, which can be heard with chest **auscultation** (listening with a stethoscope). If this fluid becomes more significant you may hear a watery or bubbling fluid sound *audibly*, without a stethoscope. These patients need rapid intervention and transport. Other signs of CHF can include swelling of the ankles, known as **pedal edema**, **jugular vein distention** (JVD) of their neck veins, and general **edema** (fluid in the tissues.) **Pitting edema** is a sign of fluid in the tissues, when swollen tissue, often in the legs, leaves a "pit" or dent when pushed on. CHF patients should be kept sitting up and often experience **orthopnea** (difficulty breathing when lying down). These patients often require **positive pressure** breathing to force air into the lungs.

If a patient you have sitting up for some reason suddenly becomes unresponsive, you should then lay them down, and assess them for pulse and breathing.

Pneumothorax/Tension pneumothorax:

A **pneumothorax** is usually from trauma, causing air to leak into and build up in the chest cavity, that then pushes on the lung; if it becomes worse, it can become a **tension pneumothorax**, completely collapsing the lung, and putting pressure on the trachea causing **tracheal deviation**, and on the aorta causing low blood pressure. *These are medical emergencies, requiring high-flow oxygen and/or positive pressure assisting of breathing and rapid transport.*

Sucking chest wound:

A hole into the chest cavity, puncturing the lung, with air and/or blood moving in and out of the wound with breaths. Generally, treatment is covering the wound with an occlusive dressing (plastic or Vaseline gauze) to seal the area. If the patient becomes worse after this treatment, we may be causing a *tension pneumothorax* and the occlusive dressing should then be removed. *High-flow oxygen or assist with bag mask device and rapid transport.*

The brain: (The neurologic system)

The brain is very sensitive to a loss of oxygen. The brain begins to die if deprived of oxygen for more than 4-6 minutes. Death of brain cells is permanent. There are several lobes of the brain, and each lobe is mostly responsible for some specific functions.

A *stroke* is a brain problem. A stroke is caused by either a clot blocking an artery (*thrombolytic* stroke) or the rupture of an artery (a *hemorrhagic* stroke.) Either type of stroke will keep oxygenated blood from reaching a portion of the brain, usually resulting in brain damage to that area. Typically, the stroke patient experiences slurred speech, headache, and one-sided weakness or paralysis. The effects of a stroke may be slight or significant and can sometimes be reversed with rapid intervention. A "clot-busting" medication might dissolve a clot and even reverse the effects of the stroke, if given quickly. Rapid transport to a *stroke center*, if possible, is important. Most often the stroke patient will require significant time and therapy to regain proper speech or movement and may suffer permanent effects. We should normally keep our stroke patients *sitting up*, to avoid additional pressure on the brain. Sitting straight up is known as *"fowler's position."*

Headaches, blurred vision, dizziness, could also be a sign of a brain tumor, or numerous other medical problems.

The abdomen:

We divide the *abdominal quadrants* into four. Using the umbilicus (belly button) as the dividing line, we have the right and left upper quadrants (RUQ, LUQ) and the right and left lower quadrants (RLQ, LLQ.)

Right upper quadrant: liver, gallbladder, part of the pancreas
Left upper quadrant: stomach, spleen, part of the pancreas
Right lower quadrant: appendix, ovary, fallopian tube, colon
Left lower quadrant: ovary, fallopian tube, colon

Diverticulitis: abnormal pouches in the intestine, causing pain.

Cholecystitis: inflammation of the *gallbladder*, causing nausea and vomiting, especially after eating greasy foods, fever, RUQ pain, pain radiating to right shoulder, often known as "**referred pain.**"

Appendicitis: Inflammation/infection of the appendix, RLQ

Dissecting aortic aneurysm: a ballooning of the aorta, felt as a pulsating mass, usually from artery disease causing weakness. Do not push on it!

The endocrine system:

The *endocrine system* is a collection of glands that produce *hormones* and excrete them directly into the circulatory system. It includes the pineal gland, pituitary gland, *pancreas*, ovaries, testes, thyroid gland, and adrenal glands. The *hypothalamus*, in the brain, is the control center for the *endocrine system*. The EMT's knowledge of the endocrine system will probably be limited. We should know that the *pancreas* is where *insulin* is produced.

Perfusion/Shock:

Perfusion means getting oxygenated blood to all the vital organs and tissues of the body. It is largely related to our blood pressure, and the proper functioning of our vessels. If we are not adequately perfusing, we are usually in some degree of *shock*. Shock is widespread inadequate perfusion. Treatment for shock is usually accomplished by placing the patient *supine* (on their back) and might include elevating their legs to increase blood flow to the brain. If a patient is dizzy, or confused, we should consider placing them in shock position. If we suspect a *stroke*, we should check their blood pressure first, if it is high, we should keep them sitting up, NOT in shock position.

Positions:

We've talked about *supine*, flat on the back. *Fowler's*, sitting straight up, and *shock position*, on the back with the feet elevated. If our patient is confused *(Altered Level Of Consciousness)*

ALOC, we should place them on their side, in *recovery position*, to protect their airway in the event of vomiting. The *left side is preferred*, since the seating in the ambulance will then have them facing us, and, placement on the left side makes it less likely they will vomit, due to the position of the valve in the stomach. Placement on their left side is known as the *left-lateral* position.

So, we have some general "position" rules:

Trouble breathing (SOB) shortness of breath: *sit them up*
Possible stroke/High blood pressure: *sit them up*
Nausea/Vomiting: *sit them up*
Possible head injury with intercranial pressure: *sit them up (or at least elevate the head) they may be on a backboard for possible spinal injury.*
Dizzy: *lay them down*
Confused: *lay them down*
Pale/cool/sweaty (shocky): *lay them down*
Unconscious: *lay them down*
Slow or no pulse: *lay them down*
Low blood pressure: *lay them down*
They took, or you're going to give nitroglycerin: *lay them down*

And, of course, we have some exceptions to the rules:

If we sit them up, then they get dizzy, or pass out, *lay them down.*

If we laid them down, then they have trouble breathing, *sit them up.*

Patient assessment: *(The exact method of doing a primary and secondary patient assessment can vary from state to state, county to county, or even from one instructor to the next. You may learn a somewhat different method, or even somewhat different names for your assessment, but the basics are quite similar.)*

Assessing the patient is perhaps THE most important EMT skill! We must consistently gather important information on *all* patients to determine the best treatment for the patient, and to allow us to give a complete report to the nurse or doctor at the hospital. We should always consider the *worst-case scenario* when treating our patients. *Better to over-treat than to under-treat.*

Patient assessments are divided into sections. Most often there is some **initial** or **primary assessment**. This is likely to include those things we consider quickly in the first moments as we arrive at the scene. This is often called the **"Scene Size-Up."** We will quickly determine if there is anything about this scene that seems unsafe, and may leave the area at that point, or not enter until police or fire personnel arrive. We will quickly determine if we should call for additional equipment or personnel. Do you see several patients? Should we call additional ambulances? If it is safe? We must pay attention to details and our surroundings as we approach the patient. We might notice their leg is bent in an odd position, or the steering wheel of the car is bent, and suspect a chest injury. We might see bleeding and will quickly examine the area and apply measures to stop any serious bleeding. We observe the details that might be important later as we give the report to the nurse or doctor, and we will need to accurately describe the situation we encountered, as we *paint a picture* of the scene for the hospital personnel.

We use many **mnemonics** in the medial field. These are letters or words that help us remember information, such as ABC's in CPR for *Airway, Breathing, Circulation.* Or, CPR, *Cardio Pulmonary Resuscitation.* There are many helpful mnemonics for the patient assessment, making it easier to remember long lists of information. Some of the mnemonics used here *I* have made up, and may not be found in other books, some are universal in most EMT training courses.

Scene size-up:

The *Scene Size-up* might include these elements, represented by the mnemonic **PENMIRE**:

Personal and scene safety
Environmental hazards and conditions

Number of patients
Mechanism of injury (how they were injured)
Immobilization (of potential spinal injuries)
Resources, additional ambulances/manpower
Equipment, specialized tools

The *Scene Size-up* is followed by the **Primary Assessment** (Initial Assessment.)

Primary Assessment:

GILT-D, **G**eneral **I**mpression, **L**ife-**T**hreats, **D**eformities

WIPEN, **W**hy we were called, **I**ntroduce yourself, **P**ermission to treat, **E**mpathy, **N**ame of patient.

AVPU, **A**lert, **V**erbal, **P**ain, **U**nresponsive

This reflects the patient's initial level of responsiveness. If they have their eyes closed until you talk to them, V, if it takes a painful stimulus to get a response, P.

*What is allowed when checking for painful response can vary. In Los Angeles County we are limited to "**inter-digital pressure**." Place a penlight between two of their fingers and squeeze the fingers against the penlight. Be careful. Practice this to see how much pressure it takes to hurt you; don't squeeze harder than that on any patient.*

A, B, C, D, E, F and **TD**, **A**irway, **B**reathing, **C**irculation, **D**isability (facial droop, slurred speech, etc.) **E**xpose (to visualize area of complaint) **F**orm a field impression (how serious this is) and make a **T**ransport **D**ecision.

Secondary Assessment:

This *initial assessment* is usually followed by a **secondary assessment**. In which we will talk to the patent, examine the patient, and determine what actions we should take. We are gathering information that helps us decide how serious this is, if rapid CODE 3 transport is required, or if time is not critical.

We may choose to do a ***rapid trauma assessment*** first, to quickly go from head-to-toe feeling for any injury. This *rapid trauma assessment* is limited to feeling for (TIC) *tenderness*, *instability*, and **crepitus** (the grating of broken bone ends.) This can be completed quickly in about one minute.

The questioning of patients should always include several key elements:

SAMPLE*:* **S**igns/**s**ymptoms, **A**llergies, **M**edications, **P**ertinent history, **L**ast oral intake, **E**vents leading to the complaint.

We can use **SAMPLE** with *every* patient to gather helpful information. We should always be *thinking*, and don't want to become robots, and we must modify our questioning when it is appropriate. Perhaps we don't need to ask about "Last oral intake" for a patient with a laceration on their finger.

*The exact way we conduct a history can vary widely depending on your school or the jurisdiction you will work in. Our questions will always vary somewhat, depending on the reason the patient called, and upon the answers to your questions. But there are several items of information we will **always** gather, such as:*

The **chief complaint**, the *main thing* that is wrong today, or why they called you. What are their signs and symptoms?

With many of the questions we will ask, we should not assume that their answer is complete; after asking why they called today, they might say they have *chest pain*. We should follow that answer with, "Is there anything else, or just this chest pain?" We will follow that same method later, when asking about medicine they take, or allergies they have; "Is that the only medicine you take?" "Are you allergic to anything else."

Their **name and age**.

A detailed description of **what happened**, as in *precisely* what were they doing if they got injured *(known as the **Mechanism of**

Injury) Or for a medical complaint, **what they were doing just before this complaint occurred.**

Do they have **any medical conditions/history** they are treated for? What are they? What treatment do they receive?

For a medical condition, ask **if they've had this before**. If they have, did they see a doctor, and what was done for them? What is this condition called?

Do they take **any medicines**? What is that medicine for?

Do they have **any allergies**?

At some point we will take *vital signs*; pulse, lung sounds and respiratory rate, blood pressure, pupil check, and assess skin signs. Before taking a blood pressure, where we would need to stop talking and have the patient be quiet in order to hear the pulse sounds, we should make sure we have asked enough questions first to gather some basic information, *then* take the blood pressure.

A *neurologic exam* seeks to assess their brain function; checking to see if they are "Alert and Oriented" **A/Ox3**, *Person, Place, Time*.

*A/Ox4, Person, Place, Time, **Purpose** (do they recall what they were doing before this happened) has been used for decades, but some places have switched to A/Ox3, for no good reason I suspect.*

You will learn to assess their **GCS**, *Glasgow Coma Score*, and to assess **PMS**, *Pulse, Motor, Sensation*, on all extremities.

Some complaints lead us to ask some other specific questions, and use specific mnemonics, such as *OPQRST* for a complaint of *chest pain* or chest discomfort.

*Sometimes a cardiac complaint is not **pain**, but might be described as pressure, or squeezing, or tightness. Don't keep using the word "pain" if **they** don't. It's best to use the 1-10 scale to have the* *patient rate their pain; ten being the worst pain they've ever had. Allow the patient to describe this pain in their own words rather than giving them choices such as sharp, stabbing, pressure, tightness, etc.*

OPQRST:

Onset: *What were they doing when this began*

Provoking factors: *Does anything make this better or worse*

Quality: *Ask them to describe how this pain feels*

Region/Radiation: *Exactly where is this pain, does it go anywhere else*

Severity: *On a scale of 1-10, ten being the worst, rate this pain*

Time: *How long have you had this today*

Remember that you will be giving a report on your findings to the doctor or nurse at the hospital. Make sure you fully understand the answers to your questions. If you asked them "How long have you had this today?" And they said "Since 6 a.m." And it's 8 p.m. now. Has this pain been present for14 hours? Maybe not. You would follow up and ask them if the pain has been constant this whole time, or has it come and gone. Make sure their answer is specific, so that your report to the doctor will be as accurate as possible.

We will assess their *level of consciousness*, generally with **AVPU**, are they **A**lert, do they only respond when you use **V**erbal stimulus, or only to **P**ainful stimulus, or are they **U**nresponsive.

At some point we will also ask our more detailed Alert and oriented times three **(A/Ox3)** questions. *Person, Place, Time.* Do they know their name, where they are, and the month and year?

For a patient with an altered level of consciousness, we can use the *AEIOU-TIPS* pneumonic to ask several key questions that often cause level of consciousness issues:

Alcohol, Epilepsy, Insulin, Overdose, Under dose, Trauma, Infection, Psychiatric conditions, and Stroke.

Of course, we may not be able to get answers to these questions from the confused or unresponsive patient and will ask these questions of friends or family if they are available.

TERMS:
Contusion = bruise
Abrasion = scrape
Laceration = cut or tear in the skin
Crepitus = movement or grating of broken bones
Asymmetry = not *symmetrical* (the same on both sides)
Racoon eyes = discoloration/bruising around the eyes like a mask
Battles sign = discoloration/bruising behind the ear/mastoid area
    Raccoon eyes and Battles sign often indicate a skull fracture
Coffee ground emesis = brown or black flakey vomit
    A sign of partially digested blood, a bleed in or above the stomach
Soot = blackening caused by smoke
Jugular veins = large veins in the neck
Carotid pulse = pulse in the neck at the carotid artery
C-7 = the seventh cervical vertebra at the back of the neck
Accessory muscle = muscles used when breathing is difficult
Tracheal deviation = trachea is pushed off to one side, not centered
    One of the signs of a tension pneumothorax
Track marks = scaring on the skin over veins from IV drug use
    Feel tattoos, they may hide track marks
Subcutaneous emphysema = air under the skin
    Check for in neck, chest, abdomen, and back
Stoma = *surgical hole* in the neck to create an airway
Paradoxical chest movement = area of a wound on the chest that
    moves in with inhalation, and puffs out with exhalation
Sucking chest wound = air going in and out of a chest wound
Distention = swelling or puffing out of an area
Rigidity = a stiff or hard area that would normally be soft
Guarding = tensing up, or protecting a sensitive or painful area
Masses = an unusual lump or object felt on palpation
Priapism = constant erection in a male, sometimes related to spinal
    injury

Incontinence = loss of bowel or bladder control
Femoral pulse = pulse in the groin
Pedal pulse = pulse in the feet
Fistula = surgical union of vein and artery in arm for dialysis
Renal = refers to the kidneys
Sacral/sacrum = near the lowest area of the spine

The Detailed Physical Exam: (The names of these assessments may vary)

A "head-to-toe" or ***Detailed physical exam*** of our patient is often needed in the case of serious trauma. For serious trauma, or possible hidden injuries, we sometimes get our patients ***trauma naked***. We may remove or cut off ALL their clothing if their *mechanism of injury* is such that we suspect possible hidden injuries. A stab, or gunshot, or other puncture wound may be small and hard to see. Patients may believe they have been stabbed or shot *one* time, when they have *several* wounds.

Patients with other painful injuries may not realize they have additional injuries, until we touch the area. In such cases, after getting them *trauma naked*, you must carefully look and feel for such hidden wounds. We should be sensitive to leaving a patient exposed in public and cover them back up after our exam.

We will have *some* detailed method of checking each area of the body, and of looking for some specific things in each of those areas. The exact method of this exam may vary in different areas of the country.

An example of a *detailed physical exam*, or *head-to-toe exam* might be something like this:

Head:
Assess for: **DCAP-BLS**, **D**eformities, **C**ontusions, **A**brasions, **P**enetrations/**P**unctures, **B**urn/**B**ruises, **L**acerations, **S**welling/**S**cars.
Palpate for: **TIC**, **T**enderness, **I**nstability, **C**repitus.

*This **assessment** (generally a visualization) and **palpation** (feeling for) is repeated for every area of the body, skipping **TIC** in the abdomen where there are no bones to palpate.*

Additional assessment of the head: **ARDS**, **A**symmetry, **R**acoon eyes/Battles sign, **D**rainage/including Coffee ground emesis, **S**oot/singed nasal or facial hair.

Neck:
DCAP-BLS and TIC
Additional assessment of the neck: **MJ-CCATTS**, **M**edical tags, **J**ugular Vein Distention, **C**arotid pulse/**C**-7 prominence, **A**ccessory muscle use, **T**racheal deviation/**T**rack marks-Tattoos, **S**ubcutaneous emphysema/Stoma.

Chest:
DCAP-BLS and TIC
Additional assessment of the chest: **P-BASS**, **P**aradoxical chest wall movement, **B**reath sounds, **A**ccessory muscle use, **S**ucking chest wounds/**S**ubcutaneous emphysema.

Abdomen:
DCAP-BLS
Additional assessment of the abdomen: **DR-GMPS**, **D**istention, **R**igidity, **G**uarding, **M**asses, **P**regnancy signs, **S**ubcutaneous emphysema.

Pelvis:
DCAP-BLS and TIC
Additional assessment of the pelvis: **PPIB-F**, **P**riapism/**P**regnancy signs, **I**ncontinence, **B**leeding, **F**emoral pulses.

Lower extremities:
DCAP-BLS and TIC
Additional assessment of the lower extremities: **PMTS**, **P**edal Pulses, **M**otor movement/**M**edical tags, **T**rack marks/**T**attoos, **S**ensation.

Upper extremities:
DCAP-BLS and TIC
Additional assessment of the upper extremities: **PMTS**, **P**ulses (brachial/radial), **M**otor movement/**M**edical tags, **T**rack marks/**T**attoos, **S**ensation. (*Fistula*, for dialysis/renal failure)

Back:
DCAP-BLS and TIC
Additional assessment of the back: **SST**, **S**acral edema/**S**ubcutaneous emphysema, **T**rack marks/**T**attoos.

BLS vs. ALS:

An EMT level patient is generally *stable*, not in serious or critical condition, and is considered a **BLS** (Basic Life Support) patient. If our patient's vital signs are abnormal, or their complaint is *chest pain* or *trouble breathing*, life-threatening trauma, or any condition where Paramedics may have some advanced treatment, medication, or special equipment, it should be considered an **ALS** (Advanced Life Support) or *Paramedic* call, and we should request them immediately if not already dispatched to the call.

The Glasgow Coma Score *(Normal 4-5-6)*

*A low **GCS** score may be a predictor of a serious brain injury, and is mostly a data element, not something that necessarily changes our emergency care. A low GCS does indicate rapid transport.*

Eye Opening
Stimuli needed for patient to open eyes
      4 = spontaneous
      3 = responds to voice
      2 = responds only to painful stimuli
      1 = no response

Verbal Response
Best communication when questioned

     5 = oriented, converses normally
     4 = confused, disoriented
     3 = inappropriate words or phrases
     2 = incomprehensible sounds
     1 = makes no sound

Motor Response
Best response to command or stimulus

     6 = obeys commands
     5 = localizes stimulus (purposeful)
     4 = flexion, withdraws from stimulus
     3 = abnormal flexion (spastic) (*decorticate posturing*)
     2 = extension (rigid) (*decerebrate posturing*)
     1 = makes no movement

A perfect GCS score is 15.
The worst score, with no responses, is 3.

Pages 17-36 covered a LOT of basic information you need to know. You read it, but how much of that did you retain? You'll need to *know* this information, not just read it. On page 155-165 you'll find 192 questions based on information found on pages 17-36, try to answer those questions. How much of that did you learn? You'll need to read and re-read this book and take notes on particular information that may be hard to remember. Writing down information is another way to make it stick in your head, along with repetition and lots of STUDY. Study equals TIME. Use the EMT Study app a LOT. Study this book and the other book listed at the end of this book. Work hard, you can do this!

*Some of the preceding information will be expanded upon or repeated in the pages that follow. This is done intentionally; **repetition is a helpful tool for remembering new information.***

Notes:

1. Packaging the patient = Preparing for transport.

2. EMD: *Emergency Medical Dispatching*: Includes 'pre-arrival' instructions on what to do, given to the caller.

3. ED: Emergency Department, or **ER**, Emergency Room.

4. Medical Director: A physician in charge of authorizing EMT's in a given jurisdiction.

5. *Medical Control*: *Offline*, through "standing orders" that allow certain procedures to be performed independently, or *Online* control requiring contact with physician or approved nurse for approval of treatments.

6. *Quality control*, or *Continuous Quality Improvement* (CQI), review of patient care and procedures by Medical Director, hospitals, agencies and companies to ensure quality and allow for improvement.

7. EMT's are *patient advocates*, our actions are done with the best interests of the patient in mind. High quality *patient care,* along with our and the patient's safety is our focus.

8. EMT's strive to maintain a professional appearance, attitude and behavior, and must be able to perform under stress and pressure with a calm composure and self-confidence.

9. EMT's must keep patient information confidential, and are bound by laws such as **HIPAA**, with which you should become familiar.

10. PSA, *primary service area.* Your area of responsibility and response.

11. The ***well-being of the EMT*** involves several factors including your personal health; vaccinations for disease prevention, getting enough sleep, proper nutrition, fitness/exercise, and emotional health. Of course, smoking or tobacco, excessive alcohol, and drug use are dangers to our health and should be avoided.

12. Safety is our first concern. *Personal* safety, *scene* safety and the safety of *others*, with patient care coming next if it is safe to do so. We should be thinking about possible exits from the area if we must leave quickly, seeking ***concealment*** (making it harder to be seen) and ***cover***, using something as a physical barrier for protection.

13. Stress is an important and negative factor in this line of work. The EMT is exposed to situations that most people will never see and will never be called upon to handle. **PTSD**, *Post Traumatic Stress Disorder* is a real risk for emergency workers. Sometimes **CISM**, *Critical Incident Stress Management* programs will help to deal with a particularly stressful or traumatic incident, with the help of counselling or group sessions where co-workers can share their thoughts. The EMT can help to reduce the impact of such stressors by having outside hobbies, not working too much overtime, and practicing various techniques to help with relaxation. *The EMT should seek professional help if the negative signs of stress occur.*

14. Safe lifting: Have sufficient help, don't strain yourself. Plan the lift, bend at the knees not the waist, keep the weight close to you, lift with your legs, don't bend your back.

15. Infectious diseases: An infectious disease spreads harmful organisms (pathogens) within the body. A *communicable disease* can be spread between people. To help avoid exposure to pathogens we can use **PPE's**, Personal Protective Equipment, such as gloves, mask, goggles, gowns. Frequent handwashing is vitally important. Soiled items should be disposed of in approved biohazard bags, and non-disposable items must be properly disinfected using approved disinfectants.

16. The spread, or *transmission*, of infectious diseases can be from *direct contact (touching)* of *bloodborne* (in the blood) fluids, including sexual contact, *indirect contact* with some object the person has touched and transferred the blood or fluid, *airborne*, carried in the air, such as TB (tuberculosis), *food-borne* (in food), *vector-borne*, (carried by animals, especially rodents).

17. OSHA *(Occupational Safety and Health Administration)* publishes guidelines to reduce hazards in the workplace and to protect workers; and the **CDC** *(Centers for Disease Control and Prevention)* produces standard to follow to help prevent disease transmission.

18. EMT's should not generally handle needles. When assisting Paramedics, the Paramedic should directly dispose of the "sharp" into an approved container. Needles (sharps) should not be passed off to another person for disposal.

19. Immunizations recommended: Hepatitis B, Influenza, Measles/Mumps/Rubella (MMR) Varicella (chickenpox) and Tetanus, Diphtheria/Pertussis (Tdap).

20. Hazardous materials safety placards. Most often diamond shaped, to warn of an area or vehicle with hazardous materials present. The EMT should always be cautious of hazardous materials or conditions at the scene of an emergency call. Chemicals, weather conditions, debris, electrical lines, and other potential hazards seen, and unseen, should be considered. Proper protective clothing should be worn when available, and the EMT must consider when it is wise to leave the area and wait for properly equipped and trained personnel to handle the hazard.

21. Our **patients often present a potential danger to us** or have factors that could make them combative or difficult to handle, such as mental health issues, anxiety, pain, fear, or drug use.

22. We should **be honest with our patients**, and not tell them something that is not true or something that don't know about their condition, such as "You'll be fine." We often do not know about the ultimate outcome of an illness or injury and should not try to predict an outcome to the patient or family. "We're doing everything we can" and "The doctor at the hospital will take good care of you" is a more appropriate response.

23. The friends or family dealing with the death of a loved one often experience several steps during **the grieving process**; denial, anger/hostility, bargaining, depression, acceptance. The EMT crew should be empathetic and supportive, understanding this is a painful situation.

24. *Cultural diversity* and sensitivity. We should be professional, not use foul language to things that might cause offense or insult someone, and be thoughtful about gender, race, religion, and other issues that could be controversial, or result in someone feeling harassed.

25. Patient Care Report (PCR.) The precise names of the reports or records we keep as EMT's can vary, but we must be careful and complete when filling out these records.

26. Patients must give **consent** (approval) to be treated and transported. Consent can be **implied** if the patient cannot respond to us. If a patient is over 18 years old (an adult) and they are **alert and oriented**, and not intoxicated, they are allowed to **refuse care**, even in a possible life-threatening situation. If they have a life-threatening illness or injury, but refuse care or transport, and are a minor, or are confused, or intoxicated, the police may need to place them on a *hold* so that you can transport them. State laws vary as to what may legally be considered an **emancipated minor**, such as being married, having a child, being in the military, or even living on their own away from their parents. Become familiar with the laws in your state. If you can reach a parent or guardian, it is best to do so, if not, you are allowed to treat and transport a minor child. Usually a school may also give permission to treat and transport a student.

27. Forcibly **restraining a patient**. You must become familiar with your local laws and protocols regarding patient restraint. You <u>can</u> defend yourself if you are attacked, although our first action should usually involve leaving the area to avoid a confrontation.

28. Advanced directives: A will, power of attorney, health care proxy, or **DNR** (Do Not Resuscitate) order may give you information as to a patient's medical wishes in the event of a medical emergency. A properly filled out DNR form, or approved DNR bracelet or necklace, will allow you to follow the patient's wished and NOT resuscitate them in the event of a respiratory or cardiac arrest. Make sure you understand your local protocols regarding advanced directives.

29. Obvious signs of death (presumptive signs): You will have specific local protocols regarding your actions with a patient who seems to be dead and beyond any resuscitation efforts. **Definitive** signs of death (obvious/clear signs) are *dependent lividity* (the settling of blood in a dependent/lower part of the body) and *rigor mortis* (stiffening of the body) and *putrefaction* (decomposition of tissues.) We do not attempt CPR or other resuscitation of an obviously dead patient. **Medical Examiner (*Coroner*)** cases are often those involving an unattended death, crime, accident, suicide, poisoning, and children. We should be careful when possible not to disturb the body or items at the scene that could be important parts of an investigation.

30. Scope of practice: State law and your *Medical Director* will determine the procedures you are allowed to carry out as an EMT. You must be familiar with, and not exceed your legal scope of practice.

31. Standard of care: You are legally expected to deliver the appropriate care (standard of care) based on your license/certification, your training, and local protocols. EMT textbooks generally follow the standards established by the **NHTSA**, *National Highway Transportation Safety Administration*. Your local protocols, developed by your local

EMS authority and Medical Director, are your primary guide for your expected standard of care.

32. Duty to act: Citizens without a medical license or certification are not required to help in the event of a medical emergency. On duty, you *are*, and your local rules may require you to act even when off duty. You could be found guilty of ***negligence*** if you have a duty to act and fail to, or if you do not perform according to expected standards, and if the patient is harmed, and it is shown that your actions or lack of action caused the harm. (Showing that you caused the harm is known as ***proximate causation***.)

33. Abandonment: You are responsible for your patient. You cannot leave your patient unattended; you must make sure that you properly transfer the care of your patient to another appropriate medical professional who is at least equally competent before leaving them. This transfer should include a report on the patient's complaint and the results of your assessment of the patient.

34. Assault: putting a person in fear of bodily harm, or even threatening to restrain them. **Battery**: unlawfully touching someone without consent. **False imprisonment** or **kidnapping**: taking someone by force, or not letting them leave if they no longer agree to be transported.

35. Good Samaritan Laws: Laws intended for the general public, who are encouraged to offer help to someone having a medical emergency. Usually protects against a successful lawsuit, even if some harm was done by the "Good Samaritan." These laws generally hold the person helping to the standard of doing what some other reasonable person might have done in that situation. *As an EMT, you will always be held to the standard of what a similarly trained EMT would have done.*

36. Record-keeping: We must keep accurate and complete records, following all your local requirements. These records become **legal documents** that might be used in court. You may have special reporting requirements regarding child and elder abuse, reporting certain crimes or injuries, such as gun shot wounds, drug related injuries, communicable diseases, childbirth, rape, domestic violence, even dog bites. You must be familiar with local reporting requirements. *The EMT becomes a **mandated reporter** of possible child abuse situations.*

37. Crime scene: Be cautious not to disturb or damage potential evidence at the scene when possible. Make note of, or even drawings of, anything you move or touch and report that to law enforcement. Try not to disturb footprints, bullet casings, weapons, and don't cut through bullet or stab wounds in clothing if possible.

38. Ethics: right and wrong, **Morality**: character and conscience, **Bioethics**: ethical decisions in the healthcare setting. We must have the highest standards of behavior as an EMT. *Honesty* is vital. We must immediately report wrongdoing or unethical behavior of co-workers up the appropriate chain of command. We should always make decisions based on the best interest of our patients, using logic not emotion, we must protect our patient's rights, we should always measure our decisions based on if we would agree to that decision is we were the patient, and can we defend our decision to others.

39. Communication: *Open-ended questions*, require some detail to explain, *closed-ended questions*, can be answered in short or single-word responses. Introduce yourself, get and use the patient's name, use plain language not medical terms, ask questions and wait for the answer before asking another question, show calm, confidence, and compassion, make clear decisions. Before transporting the patient, make sure they have items they might need, ID/insurance cards, house keys, glasses, and if there is anything to do around the house before you leave; turn off stove, etc. **Elderly**, speak clearly, give time to respond, don't assume they are hard of hearing. **Deaf** patients, write questions, give them paper and pen to respond, don't shout, ask questions with short answers **Blind** patients, don't speak loudly, if you lead them be careful of steps, curbs, bumping their head getting into the ambulance. **Non-English**, use neighbor, children, or 9-1-1 for interpreter. **Patient report to hospital**, give patient's name, age, chief complaint (main problem) medical history/medications, your treatment and their response, vital signs.

40. Patient report: Fill out completely, neatly. Errors, draw one line through error, add correct information. Don't block out or erase errors. Clearly document any unusual situation, refusal of care, injury caused by EMT's during treatment or transport. Report any unusual situations, especially any injuries to the patient during your treatment or transport, to supervisors.

41. Communication equipment: EMT's will usually have several forms of communication, radios, cell phones, and hard-wired telephone lines. You will have some method to contact your assigned **Base Station Hospital**, and perhaps a way to contact other responding units. Become familiar with the equipment you use. A *simplex* radio requires a push button to talk, and the release of the button to listen. *Duplex* systems allow simultaneous talk and listen. An **MDT** (Mobile Data Terminal) is a small computer, to receive or send messages.

42. Medical terminology: A *root word* is the stem, or main part of a word, such as **cardi** (heart), **hepat** (liver), **nephr** (kidney), **neur** (nerves), **psych** (mind), **thorac** (chest). A *prefix* comes before the root word, such as **hyper** (excessive, high). **hypo** (below normal, less than). **tachy** (rapid, fast), **pre** (before), **post** (after). A *suffix* appears at the end of a root word, such as **al** or **ic** (pertaining to), **algia** (pain), **ectomy** (surgical removal),
itis (inflammation), **logy** (study of), **logist** (specialist), **megaly** (enlargement), **meter** (measurement device), **oma** (tumor), **pathy** (disease). *Some prefixes that describe positions*, **ab** (away from), **ad** (toward), **circum/peri** (around), **trans** (through), **epi/supra** (above), **retro** (behind), **sub** (under), **infra** (below, under), **para** (near, beyond, beside), **contra** (against, opposite), **ecto** (outside), **endo/intra** (within), **ipsi** (same).

43. Directional terms: **anterior** (front), **posterior** (back), **superior** (top, or above some landmark), **inferior** (bottom, or below some landmark), **proximal** (closer to point of attachment), **distal** (further from point of attachment), **medial** (closer to midline), **distal** (further from midline), **superficial** (closest to skin surface), **deep** (further from skin surface). **Ventral** can mean 'belly side' and **Dorsal** can mean spinal side or posterior; we generally use *anterior* and *posterior* instead of ventral/dorsal. **Palmar** (palm of hand), **plantar** (bottom of foot). **Flexion** (bending a joint), **extension** (straightening a joint), **adduction** (movement toward midline), **abduction** (movement away from midline). **Bilateral** (both sides), **quadrants** (the abdomen divided into four quadrants at the umbilicus) RUQ, RLQ, LUQ, LLQ.

44. The Anatomical position: The parts of the body are described while picturing the body facing forward with the palms facing outward.

45. Prone: lying face down. **Supine**: lying face up. **Fowler's position**: sitting straight up. **Semi-fowler**: sitting at a 45-degree angle. **Recovery position**: lying on the side, arm above head with head resting on arm, top leg bent to prop the person in this position.

46. Skeletal system: *206 bones.* **Ligaments**, fibrous tissues that connect bone to bone. **Tendons** connect muscle to bone. **Cartilage**, smooth connective tissue that covers and cushions bone ends at joints. **Cranium**, the skull. **Foramen magnum**: a hole at base of skull where spinal cord passes through. **Occiput** or **occipital**, posterior area of cranium. **Temporal**, around the ears. **Parietal**, upper sides of the skull, right and left. **Frontal**, forehead. **Maxillae**, non-moveable jawbone. **Mandible**, moveable jaw. **Zygomas**, cheek bones. **Orbit**, eye socket.

47. Spinal column: *33 vertebrae. From top to bottom, the five sections: Cervical (7) Thoracic (12) Lumbar (5), Sacrum (5 fused), Coccyx (5 fused.)* Between each vertebra is a cushion, called the **intervertebral disc**.

48. The **thorax** is the chest area, containing *heart, lungs, esophagus*, and the *great vessels* (the aorta and vena cavae) and the *twelve pairs of ribs*. Down the midline of the chest is the **sternum**, the top border of the sternum is called the **sternal notch**, where the trachea can be felt. The small tip of cartilage at the bottom of the sternum is called the **xiphoid process.**

49. Joints are where bones come together, this is called **articulation**. The inner lining of joints is called the **synovial membrane**, and **synovial fluid** allows lubrication for movement of joints. The shoulder is an example of a **ball and socket joint**, and the knee is a **hinge joint**. *Ligaments* keep joints from bending too far.

50. The **upper extremities** are the arms. The **shoulder girdle** is where *clavicle (collar bone) scapula (shoulder blade)* and *humerus* come together. The **humerus** is the upper arm bone, the **radius** and **ulna** are the bones of the lower arm. The *radius* is on the thumb side and is larger than the *ulna*, which is on the same side as the little finger. There are *eight bones in the wrist* called the **carpal bones**. The *five bones of the hand* are the **metacarpals**, the finger bones are called the **phalanges**. The thumb has two phalanges, the fingers each have three.

51. The pelvis. The *pelvic bone*, is formed by the fusion of the **ilium** (the large top section) the **ischium** (the bottom bone, the lowest area we sit on is called the **ischial tuberosity**) and the **pubis** (that comes together at the pubic area forming the **pubic symphysis**.) The area of the pelvis where the leg connects to the hip joint is called the *acetabulum or pelvic girdle.*

52. The **lower extremities.** The **femur** is the *thighbone* and is the longest bone in the body. The top (superior) end of the femur is called the **femoral head**, which connects into the *acetabulum*. The **hip** area is formed by the top of the femur bone, the *greater trochanter*, and area below it called the *lesser trochanter*. The **knee** has a moveable boney cap over it called the **patella** (kneecap.) The lower leg bones are the **tibia** (shinbone) and **fibula**. *The fibula is the smaller lower leg bone.* The **ankle** is a hinge joint, the foot has seven **tarsal bones**, the **calcaneus** is the *heel bone*. The middle of the foot is formed by the five **metatarsal bones**. The bottom of the foot is called the **plantar surface**, the top is the **dorsum**. The toes have fourteen *phalanges*, the **great toe** has two, and each of the other toes has three.

53. The skeletal system. These bones provide the *shape* of the body, provide *protection* for delicate organs, and allow *movement*. The bones of the skeleton store *calcium*, and the interior of bones, *the bone marrow, create red blood cells, white blood cells, and platelets.*

54. The musculoskeletal system. The *bones and* voluntary *muscles*. There are *more than 600 muscles* in the musculoskeletal system. *Three types of muscles*, **skeletal** (attaches bones to the skeleton) **smooth** (within blood vessels and intestines) **cardiac** (the specialized heart muscle.) Muscles are either **voluntary** (under our control) or **involuntary** (such as the heart, that work independently.) The work of muscles produces heat, when you get cold muscles may *shiver*, which helps to produce needed heat.

55. The respiratory system includes all the body structures related to breathing; *nose, mouth, throat, larynx, trachea, bronchi, bronchioles, lungs, diaphragm, and muscles of the chest.* **Accessory muscles** are various muscles that support breathing, and when noticeable may indicate difficulty breathing, such as strained neck, chest, or abdominal muscles; this is called *labored breathing*. **The upper airway** is the airway above the **larynx** (voice box) including the *nose, mouth, tongue, jaw, pharynx, larynx*. The *larynx* is very sensitive to fluid or objects and will contract from any foreign object and may lead to **laryngospasm**, closing off the airway. The **oropharynx** includes the mouth and ends at the larynx. The **nasopharynx** leads from the nose to the structures above the roof of the mouth and leads to the *oropharynx*. At the bottom of the **pharynx** are the **trachea** (windpipe) the main airway, and the **esophagus**, leading to the stomach. The **epiglottis** is a thin flap that protects the *trachea* from food or liquid. **Thyroid cartilage** (Adam's apple) is the anterior part of the *larynx*. The **vocal cords** are contained in the *larynx*. Just below the *thyroid cartilage* is the **cricoid cartilage**, between the *thyroid* and *cricoid* cartilage is the **cricothyroid membrane**, which is a landmark for an ALS procedure to gain access to the airway with a needle and a small airway. Below the *cricoid cartilage* is the **trachea**, which branches into the **right and left** *bronchi*, which branch into smaller and smaller airways within each lung, until reaching millions of the smallest airways the **alveoli**, which are small grape-like structures where oxygen enters the blood stream and carbon dioxide is removed through capillaries.

56. The **pleura,** is a thin membrane cover each lung. The pleura sits next to a similar membrane in the chest, slipping against each other, allowing movement as the chest wall expands, pulling the lungs with it, creating a *negative pressure* which causes air to enter the nose and mouth. The **pleural space** is a *potential space*, meaning it doesn't exist unless some problem occurs allowing blood, other fluid, or air to enter. The **diaphragm** separates the *thorax* from the *abdomen*, and pulls the lungs down during *inhalation*, to increase the pressure and negative space, allowing for greater lung expansion. The *diaphragm* is unique, being both an *involuntary* and *voluntary* muscle. The *muscles involved in breathing are* the *neck* (cervical) muscles, the *pectoral* muscles of the chest, the *intercostal* muscles (between the ribs) the *abdominal* muscles, and the *diaphragm.*

57. *Physiology* **of the respiratory system:** The purpose of the respiratory system is to get oxygen to the body and to remove carbon dioxide. **Ventilation** is the movement of air into and out of the lungs. **Respiration** is the gas exchange to and from the cells. **Diffusion** is the movement of molecules from an area of *higher concentration to an area of lower concentration, though semi-permeable membranes* (so thin that molecules can pass through the membrane). There are more *oxygen* molecules in the air than in the bloodstream, therefore oxygen moves into the blood. There are more *carbon dioxide* molecules in the blood than in the air (of the alveoli) therefore carbon dioxide moves out of the blood and into the alveoli to be exhaled. Room air contains about 21% *oxygen*, exhaled air about 16% oxygen and 3-5% *carbon dioxide, nitrogen* makes up about 79% of air, and is *inert*, which means we do not use it. Our breathing is regulated largely in the brain, where the *medulla oblongata* in the brain stem, senses PH levels in the CSF, *cerebral spinal fluid* (in this case *acid build up* from *excessive* *carbon dioxide*) and stimulates the **phrenic nerve** which stimulates the *diaphragm* to increase its contractions and to exhale more carbon dioxide, to reduce the PH level. A secondary system to control respirations takes place when sensors in the *brain, aorta,* and *carotid arteries* can sense *low oxygen levels.* This system is much less sensitive than the CO2 (carbon dioxide) sensors in the brain stem.

58. Ventilation: *Tidal volume* is the amount of air breathed in, or breathed out, in one breath. We estimate if this is adequate and give artificial ventilation if we believe it is not adequate. We assess the *rate* of breathing (breaths per minute) *tidal volume,* along with *accessory muscle use* and *skin signs* (cyanosis) *mentation* (ability to think and respond) all taken together to determine if breathing is adequate.

58. Children and breathing: Children's airways are smaller and more delicate, and their tongues are larger; making children, especially infants, more susceptible to airway complications. *Signs of breathing distress in infants and children* may include; *accessory muscle use or retraction in the neck and chest, nasal flaring, seesaw breathing* (alternating between using chest and abdominal muscles when breathing) and *grunting with breaths*, are all dangerous signs indicating serious breathing distress and the need for rapid intervention and rapid transport.

60. *The normal breathing rate* for adults is about 12 times per minute. Children often breath faster, up to 40 times per minute, and infants generally breath about 30-60 times per minute. **Agonal gasps**, or **agonal breathing**, is sometimes referred to as "dying breaths" and may be seen immediately after a *cardiac arrest.* These last gasps will usually be slow and shallow, and will be very irregular, and there will only be a few until they stop breathing completely.

61. The circulatory system *or* **Cardiovascular system:** The organs and vessels that carry blood. Arteries carry oxygenated blood from the heart and branch into arterioles, then into capillaries, then take the deoxygenated blood into venules, then veins and back to the heart.

62. The heart: This muscle, called the **myocardium**, is about the size of a fist, is actually two pumps side by side. The dividing membrane between the left and right side is called the **septum**. The two upper pumping chambers are the **atria**, the two bottom chambers are the **ventricles**. *The left side is the high-pressure side and pumps to the body, the right side pumps to the lungs.* The **aorta** first branches off into the **coronary arteries** to supply the heart muscle with oxygenated blood, then carries oxygenated blood to the rest of the body. (See page 17).

63. *Normal heart rate*, is from 60 to 100 beats per minute. Each beat of the heart pumps about 70-80 mL (cc's) of blood, pumping the body's **entire blood volume of about 5-6 liters** in only one minute. The amount of blood pumped in one beat of the heart is called **stroke volume**. The amount pumped in one minute is called **cardiac output**.

64. Electrical conduction through the heart: Specialized pathways carry electrical impulses, controlling the heartbeat. Specialized **pacemaker nodes** create an electrical impulse. This begins high in the atria in the **sinoatrial node**, travels to the **atrioventricular node** to the **bundle of His**, to the **Purkinje fibers** and to the ventricles. A disruption of any of these nodes or pathways can result in abnormal cardiac rhythms, even ventricular fibrillation and death.

65. Arteries: The largest artery is the **aorta**, other specific arteries supply oxygenated blood to certain organs; **hepatic** to the *liver*, **renal** to the *kidneys*, **mesenteric** to the *digestive system*. Arteries branch off smaller and smaller until they become *arterioles* and then become *capillaries*. At the organs being oxygenated, the blood then begins heading back to the heart, first in capillaries, then though the smallest veins called venules, then into veins, then into the largest veins called the vena cava.

66. The pulses: *carotid* (in the neck) *femoral* (in the groin) *radial* (in the wrist) *brachial* (in the arm) *posterior tibial* (behind the ankle bone) *dorsalis pedis* (in the foot).

67. Veins: Largest veins are the **vena cava**, bringing *deoxygenated* blood back to the heart. The **superior vena cava** carry blood *from the head, neck, shoulders, and upper extremities.* The **inferior vena cava** carries blood *from the abdomen, pelvis, and lower extremities.* The *superior* and *inferior vena cava* merge and empty blood into the *right atrium* that is then pumped to the *lungs.* Blood vessels can *constrict* or *dilate*, often causing increased or decreased *blood pressure.* Bleeding from veins is a steady flow, bleeding from an artery will pulse with each beat of the heart.

68. The spleen. A *solid organ* under the lower rib in the *left upper part of the abdomen.* The spleen *filters* the blood, *makes blood* cells, and assists in the body's *immune response*; it is very vascular and prone to injury and serious bleeding in the event of trauma.

69. Plasma is the liquid portion of the blood; it is mostly water and proteins; CO_2 converts into *carbonic acid* and is carried by plasma. **Red blood cells** (erythrocytes) contain *hemoglobin*, which carries oxygen. **White blood cells** (leukocytes) help the bodies *immune* response to fight infections. **Platelets** help *clotting*.

70. *Physiology* **of the circulatory system**: *Blood pressure* is determined by the force of the *left ventricle* pumping blood into the *aorta*, called **systole**, which is the *top blood pressure number.* During *relaxation*, **diastole**, the left ventricle refills with blood, and gives us the *bottom blood pressure number.* The *blood pressure cuff* or other blood pressure device is called the **sphygmomanometer**. *Adults have about 6 liters of blood, children about 2-3 liters*, and *infants about 300 milliliters* (cc's.) **Perfusion** is a term to describe *adequate oxygenated blood* reaching the bodies vital organs and systems. Widespread inadequate perfusion is called **shock** or *hypoperfusion*.

71. The *nervous system* has controls two main effects on the *cardiovascular system* through the **sympathetic** and

parasympathetic systems. The *sympathetic nervous system* sends signals to the **adrenal glands** causing the release of two hormones, **epinephrine** (adrenaline) and **norepinephrine** (noradrenaline.) This stimulates the heart and blood vessels, through the **alpha-adrenergic receptors** and **beta-adrenergic receptors**, causing beneficial effects to deal with stress, known as the *fight or flight reaction. (Adrenergic refers to the adrenal gland)* Fight or flight prepares the body to react in a dangerous situation, to fight, or run, increasing heart and respiratory rate, dilating the pupils to increase vision, and increasing the use of glucose in the cells. The *alpha receptors cause constriction of vessels* increasing blood pressure. The *beta receptors are in the heart and lungs.* **Beta-1** stimulation *increases heart rate and heart contractility* (force of contraction.) **Beta-2** stimulation *causes the bronchi in the lungs to dilate*, allowing more available oxygen. These alpha and beta effects prepare the body for a *fight or flight response.* The **parasympathetic system** also effects the heart and vessels but in an opposite way, working together to control and mediate the *fight or flight response. Parasympathetic* stimulation <u>slows the heart and makes it beat more weakly</u> and moves blood to other areas; eating for example, is aided by this *parasympathetic* response. **Baroreceptors**, found in the *arch of the aorta* and the *carotid arteries*, <u>detect blood pressure changes</u> allowing the cardiovascular system to regulate perfusion.

72. The nervous system *anatomy and physiology*: The **central nervous system** is the *brain and spinal cord.* The *peripheral nervous system* are the nerves outside the brain and spinal cord that link to the organs of the body. The **somatic nervous system** is the network of nerves under *voluntary* control. The **autonomic nervous system** controls the non-voluntary, or *automatic* functions of the body.

73. The brain: <u>The three main areas of the brain</u>; *cerebrum, cerebellum,* and *brain stem.* **Cerebrum**, largest part of the brain, called the *gray-matter*, has four lobes, **frontal, parietal, temporal, occipital**. Has most to do with our intellect and personality. **Cerebellum**, under the cerebrum, called the *little brain*, controls *coordination* and *movements* of the body. The **brain stem** is the lowest area of the brain, controlling all *essential life functions* such as *cardiac*, *respirations*, and *consciousness*. An area in the brain stem known as the **reticular activating system** keeps us awake. Blood drains from the head through the jugular veins.

74. Cerebral spinal fluid (CSF): Filters out impurities and toxins, cushions the brain by absorbing shock. CSF leaking from the ears or nose indicates a skull fracture.

75. The spinal cord is an extension of the brain stem, transmitting information to and from the brain. At the level of the neck these spinal nerves cross, which is why an injury to the right side of the brain affects the left side of the body, and vice-versa.

76. The integumentary system (the skin): <u>The skin is the largest organ of the body</u>. The skin protects the body in the environment, regulates temperature, and transmits information about the environment to the brain. The skin has two parts, the **epidermis** and the **dermis**. The *epidermis* is several layers of cells, the upper most is dead cells, below that the *germinal layer* of the epidermis creates new cells and contains the *pigment* (color) of the skin. Below the *epidermis* is the **dermis**, containing *sweat glands*, *sebaceous* (oil) *glands*, *hair follicles*, *blood vessels*, and *nerve endings*. Below the dermis is the **subcutaneous layer**, which is mostly fat. The *orifices* of the body are not covered by skin, but instead my **mucous membranes**. A *mucous membrane* stays moist, the skin is generally dry. Constriction of blood vessels in a cold environment reduces heat loss, and dilation of blood vessels in a hot environment helps to radiate away heat.

77. The digestive system: (The gastrointestinal system) = stomach and intestines, mouth, salivary glands, pharynx, esophagus, liver, gallbladder, pancreas, rectum, and anus.

78. The abdomen: The **diaphragm** separates the *thorax* from the *abdomen*. The **umbilicus** (belly button) is used to divide the abdomen into four "quadrants." **RUQ** has the *liver*, *gallbladder*, and some of the *colon*. **LUQ** contains the *stomach*, *spleen*, and some of the *colon*. **RLQ** has some large and small *intestine*, *colon*, and the *appendix*. **LLQ**, *intestines*. The **bladder** is behind the *symphysis pubis* (where the lower pelvis joins at the pubic area) which also puts it in part of both lower quadrants. The *retroperitoneal area* is outside and behind the abdominal cavity and contains the **kidneys** and **pancreas**. (The *pancreas* is outside of the abdominal cavity, but in the area of both upper quadrants.)

79. The mouth: The roof of the mouth contains the **hard palate** anteriorly, and the **soft palate** posteriorly. The **salivary glands** produce *saliva*, to aid in chewing as a lubricant along with some digestive enzymes. The **oropharynx** is the area inside the mouth, ending at the *esophagus* and *trachea*.

80. The esophagus carries food to the stomach. The **pancreas** is a *solid organ* that has two types of glands, one to produce *enzymes* to help digestion, the other produces *insulin* and *glucagon* to regulate glucose (sugar) in the blood.

81. The liver: The largest *solid organ* in the abdomen, it eliminates some of the body's poisonous byproducts, is important for clotting and plasma production, as well as proper immunities, creates *bile* for digestion, and stores sugar and starch for energy. The liver has a large blood supply, making an injury to the liver particularly life-threatening.

82. The small intestine: About 90% of digestion occurs here, with 5-10% occurring in the *large intestine*.

83. The rectum, is the end of the *colon*, with circular *sphincter muscles* to control the escape of liquids, gasses, and solids from the digestive tract.

84. The lymphatic system: Helps get rid of toxins in the body, along with aiding the *immune system*. The *lymphatic system* is made up of the *spleen*, *lymph nodes*, *lymph*, *lymph vessels*, and *thymus gland*.

85. The endocrine system: Controlled by the brain, *glands that produce hormones* into the bloodstream to control various bodily functions. **Adrenal gland**, above kidneys, produces *epinephrine/norepinephrine*, stress response/fight or flight. **Ovaries**, female sexual functions, produces *estrogen*. **Pancreas**, regulates glucose, makes *insulin/glucagon*. **Pituitary**, at the base of the skull, controls all other endocrine glands. **Testes**, makes *testosterone*, male sexual functions. **Thyroid**, in the neck, *regulates metabolism*.

86. The urinary system: To control fluid balance, eliminate waste, control PH. Kidneys, solid organs. From kidneys to ureter to bladder, exits through the urethra.

87. Reproduction: Male, *testicles* produce *hormones* and *sperm*, sperm travels through tubes called *vas deferens* then through the *urethra* in the penis. **Female**, *ovaries* produce *hormones* and *egg cells*, releasing mature egg every 28 days, which travel through *fallopian tubes* to *uterus*.

88. Cells: use oxygen and nutrients to produce chemical energy through a process called *metabolism* or *cellular respiration*. *Aerobic metabolism* is the normal metabolism when sufficient oxygen is present, and the waste produced is **carbon dioxide** and *water*. **Anaerobic metabolism** occurs when oxygen is limited and produces **lactic acid**. Excess lactic acid will kill cells. **Diffusion** allows the movement of *oxygen*, *waste*, and *nutrients* from areas of greater concentration to areas of lower concentration. **PH** is the relative *acid and base balance*; normal human PH is 7.35-7.45. The *plasma* of the blood contains *bicarbonate*, which helps to *neutralize acid*, the body also *increases breathing to blow off excess carbon dioxide*, which, during **hyperventilation** can reduce carbon dioxide too much, causing an *alkaline* state.

89. Respiratory compromise: When something occurs that decreased the ability to move gas (oxygen) effectively. *Respirations are a function* of **ventilation** (moving air) and **respiration** (exchanging gases.) A *lack of oxygen* to the body is called (**hypoxia**) while *elevated carbon dioxide* levels is called (**hypercarbia**.) Some factors causing *respiratory compromise*; the *tongue* may block the airway or diseases such as *asthma* may close airways, the muscles of breathing can be affected from diseases such as *cerebral palsy* where signals from the brain to the diaphragm are affected, *spinal trauma* to the *phrenic nerve which controls contraction of the diaphragm, trauma to the chest, unconsciousness,* and *drug overdose.* **Respiration,** *the ability to exchange gases,* will be affected if the *atmosphere* changes; smoke, altitude, chemicals may reduce the normal **21% oxygen in the air**. We **exhale about 16% oxygen, using about 5%.** *Disease* can cause mucus and *fluids in the lungs*, reducing adequate respiration.

90. Shock: *Inadequate flow of oxygenated blood to the organs and tissues.* Causes of shock: *Insufficient blood volume*, from bleeding or inability to pump blood (heart problem) or *peripheral circulation* problem, vessels dilate causing blood to pool in extremities. (Loss of **PVR,** *Peripheral Vascular Resistance*). If blood pressure drops, **baroreceptors** sense this and cause a release of *epinephrine* and *norepinephrine*, causing the *heart to beat faster and harder* and causing *blood vessels to constrict*. In **hypovolemic shock** (loss of blood volume) fluid may move from the cells and vessels (*interstitial fluid*) into the capillaries in an attempt to get more fluid to pump. In **septic** and **anaphylactic shock** fluid leaks from the capillaries, moving fluid from the *intravascular space* into the tissues (interstitial space) causing less blood to return to the heart to be pumped. All types of shock ultimately result in lack of perfusion to the cells, tissues, and organs, and will cause death if not reversed.

91. Neonate (birth to 1 month), **Infant** (1 month to 1 year). *Neonates* are mostly "**nose breathers**." Make sure a baby's nose is clear of mucous if they are having difficulty breathing or choking. Because an infant's chest is not rigid, *they use the diaphragm for breathing*, causing "**belly breathing.**" **An infant's tongue is large** and **their airway short and narrow**, making *obstructions more likely*. Lungs are small and fragile, use the correct size BVM/BMD and stop inflation when the chest rises. *Do not hyperextend the neck,* open the airway in the "sniffing position."

92. Fontanelles are the soft immature bone of the infant's skull. These bones are fused by about 18 months. A *"sunken fontanelle"* can be a sign of *dehydration*. A *bulging fontanelle* can be a sign of *increased intercranial pressure.*

93. Toddler (1-3 years), **Preschooler** (3-6 years), **School age** (6-12 years), **Adolescent** (12-18 years), **Early adults** (19-40 years), **Older adults** (61 and older).

94. Atherosclerosis: Cholesterol and Calcium form plaque, leading to obstruction of blood flow, while also causing hardening of the arteries, leading to an inability to dilate when needed to bring extra blood flow to the heart. Atherosclerosis from such plaque in the coronary arteries decreases blood to the heart muscle. The result is increased work on the heart (increased pulse) and ultimately damage and weakening of the heart.

95. Power Lift: Spreading the legs about shoulder width apart, squatting and grasping with your palms up (power grip) and bending at the knees with the back straight. Keep the weigh close to you, stand up by straightening the legs while keeping the back locked in a slight curve while tightening your abdominal muscles. When pulling a patient lying on a sheet, or log-rolling a patient, kneel down close to them to avoid bending down with your back. Do not twist your body while carrying or lifting and avoid bending at the waist. Use more people when lifting, to help distribute the load.

96. The "Diamond Carry" describes four people carrying a stretcher or backboard, all facing forward in the direction of travel, one at the front and back, and one on each side at the middle.

97. The "One-handed carry" uses four people to lift and carry a backboard, two on each side. After lifting with both hands, the people turn in the direction of travel and carry the backboard with one hand.

98. Using a "Stair Chair" to move a patient down stairs, move them *feet first*, the person at the head end facing down the stairs, the person at the feet walking backwards facing the patient. *A third person* should be close behind the person at the foot end walking backwards, to open doors, and to help guide them and offer support and balance by placing both hands on their low back as they move.

99. Coordination! When moving patients: Begin any movement of the patient with a "count" that all those involved can hear. *"Move on three. One, two, three."* Plan ahead, have adequate help, call for additional manpower when needed, don't lift a heavy load without enough help.

100. Emergency moves: There are times when we can't wait for help to arrive, and we must move the patient immediately due to danger or the need to get them to a better location to allow evaluation. We can *drag* or *pull* the patient by the arms or legs or use their clothing as grab points. We try to avoid twisting, and to keep the spine aligned during all moves. Avoid "one-person" moves unless an urgent situation requires it.

101. Special concerns when moving patients: "Geriatric" or elderly patients may have brittle bones, curved spines, fear of medical care, and delicate skin, which may require special attention and care when moving.

102. Positioning the patient: Generally, patients with *chest pain* are placed in "position of comfort." *Respiratory distress*, Fowler (sitting straight up) or Semi-Fowler (sitting at about 45%) position. *Hypotensive/Shock*, supine (flat on back). *Late stages of pregnancy*; left side. (Pregnant patient on their back may cause "Supine hypotensive syndrome" due to the weight of the baby compressing the vena cava. *Unresponsive patient*, with no spinal, hip, or pelvic injury, in "recovery position" on their left side, to better protect their airway in case of vomiting.

103. Patient assessment: The most important EMS skill is the ability to quickly and appropriately assess the patient. *(Safety is always our first concern, sometimes we cannot approach the patient, if the situation is not safe to do so.)* The assessment allows us to quickly *treat* the patient if needed, and to *prioritize* their need for transport. Our assessment begins with a **Size-up** of the scene, especially in trauma situations, taking in what is visible to determine risks and the details of what has happened. (We must always have *situational awareness*, paying attention to changing conditions around us). That initial size-up, whether trauma or medical, also includes a determination of safety issues, and the need for additional equipment or resources. The **primary assessment** is performed in the first moments of our contact with the patient, determining the need for immediate intervention. We need to *form a **general impression*** of the patient quickly, to help guide our actions. We should trust our instincts when the patient "just doesn't seem right." We then gather a **patient history**, and proceed to the **secondary assessment**, which might include taking vital signs and other assessment or treatment procedures. **Reassessment** is done to determine any changes in the patient or need for other treatment. A stable patient should be reassessed at least every 15 minutes, and unstable patient at least every 5 minutes. Exact methods of assessments can vary.

104. Symptom: a *subjective* condition the patient feels and tells you about. (Such as I have a headache). A **Sign** is an objective condition you can see or measure. We treat patients based on their signs and symptoms; we do not *diagnose* them for some particular condition.

105. Mechanism of injury (MOI) or Nature of illness (NOI). *Mechanism of injury* is what happened, *how* they were injured, and based on that, what injuries might we expect. The *Nature of illness* is what is the patient's *chief complaint* related to, trouble breathing, chest pain, etc. Patient's may have several conditions or complaints, but we should determine the *chief complaint*, the most important or most serious condition happening right now.

106. PPE (Personal Protective Equipment) Such as gloves, eye protection, special clothing. ***Standard precautions*** are those protective items determined by the CDC (Centers for Disease Control) to protect against blood-borne or airborne pathogens (diseases) in blood or bodily fluids. TB (tuberculosis) as an example, is an airborne disease, requiring the EMS crew to wear an N95 protective mask.

107. Triage/Incident command: The goal of *triage* is to, *sort* out, and determine which patients are most serious, and should be treated first. *Determining the number of patients* is one of the first priorities, that and calling for *additional equipment and personnel* to handle, treat, and transport the patients.

108. Level of consciousness (LOC): Lack of oxygen to the brain, the effect of drugs, or other physiological problems can alter a patient's level of consciousness. The patient may be unconscious, conscious but with an altered level of consciousness, or conscious and alert. We will give some type of approved stimulus, *verbal* or *painful*, and note their response to that stimuli. If the person is *alert and oriented,* they should know the answer to these orientation questions: **Person** (their name), **Place** (where they are), **Time** (month, year, approximate date), **Event** (what happened). The patient is considered **"Alert and oriented times four"** if they can answer those questions. "Alert times three" means they failed one, etc. Some jurisdictions may use A/Ox3 instead of four, eliminating 'Event.'

109. Airway: Proper breathing, and an open unobstructed (patent) airway is always a priority. Noisy breathing is a bad sign and is considered *obstructed breathing*. The "Head-Tilt-Chin-Lift" is one method to open an airway; tilting the head back by pushing down on the forehead and pulling up on the chin will move the tongue up and away from the back of the throat, possibly allowing better air flow. This maneuver should be avoided *if possible* when there is suspected neck trauma.

110. Breathing: Adequate breathing is a combination of the **rate** of breathing (breaths per minute) and **tidal volume** (the amount of air being moved.) Very **shallow** or very **deep** respirations may indicate a problem. A change in skin color (**cyanosis**=blueness) that may be widespread or may begin at the lips or nailbeds, is a sign of inadequate oxygenation. Other signs of respiratory trouble, or **labored breathing**, can be **retractions** (indentation above the clavicles or in between the ribs) the use of **accessory muscles** of respiration (in the neck, the *sternocleidomastoid* muscles,) the chest (pectoralis major muscles) and **abdominal muscles**. *Nasal flaring* in children and infants is a sign of respiratory distress, as is *grunting* with each breath. **Two- or three-word dyspnea** (able to only speak a couple or words at a time) is a sign of respiratory distress, as is sitting in **tripod position** (arms out, leaning over, head raised up,) and **sniffing position** in children with their head elevated slightly.

111. Pulse: Every **artery** in the body pulsates with each beat of the heart. We **palpate** (feel) pulses in the neck (the **carotid** artery) the wrist (the **radial** artery) and the **brachial** artery in infants less than one year old, on the medial aspect of the upper arm, just under the bicep muscle.

112. Skin color: *Hypoperfusion* (less than adequate circulation) will affect skin color. Regardless of skin pigment, parts of our skin will be pink if properly perfused (adequate circulation) and can be assessed in fingernail beds, mucous membranes of the mouth and lips, and the conjunctiva of the eyes. Poor circulation will result in grayish or bluish skin color in these areas called *cyanosis*. A yellow tinge to the skin is called *jaundice*, caused by liver malfunction, which may also turn the white part of the eye (the **sclera**) yellow.

113. Other skin signs: *Color, Temperature, Moisture*. Hot or cool skin indicates a problem. Very moist, sweaty skin (**diaphoresis**) when not related to exercise or air temperature is often a sign of a serious medical issue. **Capillary refill**, how fast the nailbeds refill with blood after being squeezed (blanched white) if delayed, can be a sign of poor perfusion. *Proper capillary refill should occur in 2 seconds or less.* (Age, health problems, medications, exposure to cold, and vasoconstriction may make this test unreliable.) Capillary refill can be checked on infants and children by pushing on their forehead, sternum, or chin.

114. External bleeding: Major bleeding should be controlled *before* addressing breathing and airway issues!

115. A *Rapid Exam* or *Rapid Trauma Assessment* should be performed quickly on a patient with significant trauma and should take 60 to 90 seconds. This check is to quickly discover hidden injuries such as bleeding or fractures.

116. The *Rapid Exam*: Is a quick check from *head to toe*, with the arms and back done last. We quickly *look for* **DCAP-BLS**: **D**eformities, **C**ontusions, **A**brasions, **P**unctures, **B**urns, **L**acerations, and **S**welling. We also *feel for* **TIC**: **T**enderness, **I**nstability, **C**repitus. (Most textbook use the DCAP-BTLS pneumonic, including "Tenderness." I have moved the *Tenderness* check into the TIC portion of the exam.

117. Crepitus: *The sound or the feeling of fractured bones grinding together.*

118. *Detailed Exam* or *Detailed Physical Assessment*: (Secondary Assessment) If life threats are discovered during the Rapid Exam you should consider *rapid transport* with other assessments done in route to the hospital. If the patient seems stable without life threats, you may choose to continue your exam to check for more potential problems. There are many variations on this detailed exam and mnemonics to remember it, this is one method:

<u>Head</u>: **ARDS**: **A**symmetry of face, **R**acoon eyes/Battles sign, **D**rainage, **S**inged facial or nasal hairs.

<u>Neck</u>: **MJ-CCATTS** (MJ-Cats): **M**edical Alert tags, **J**ugular Distention, **C**-7 prominence, **C**arotid pulses, **A**ccessory muscle use, **T**racheal Deviation, **T**rack marks and Tattoos, **S**ubcutaneous emphysema.

<u>Chest</u>: **P-BASS**: **P**aradoxical chest movement, **B**reath sounds, **A**ccessory muscle use, **S**ucking chest wound, **S**ubcutaneous emphysema.

<u>Abdomen</u>: **Dr.-GM**: **D**istention, **R**igidity, **G**uarding, **M**asses (pulsating masses)

Pelvis: **PIB-F**: **P**riapism, **I**ncontinence, **B**leeding, **F**emoral pulses.

Legs: **PMT**: **P**MS (pulse, motor, sensation) **M**edical Alert tags, **T**rack marks and **T**attoos.

Arms: **PMT-F**: **P**MS (pulse, motor, sensation) **M**edical Alert tags, **T**rack marks and **T**attoos, **F**istula.

Back: **SS**: **S**acral edema, **S**ubcutaneous emphysema.

119. Racoon eyes/Battles sign: *Racoon eyes*, mask-type bruising around both eyes. **Battle's sign**, bruising behind the ear (mastoid area.) Both can be signs of a possible skull fracture.

120. Accessory muscles: Related to signs of *respiratory distress*, the use of *accessory muscles* to assist with breathing can be strained muscles in the *neck* with each breath, *nasal flaring* especially in children, *intercostal indrawing* (sucking in of the spaces between the ribs with each inhalation) and use of *abdominal muscles* to help push the diaphragm.

121. Tracheal deviation: The trachea can be felt centered at the sternal notch, between the clavicles at the top of the sternum. If the trachea is not centered, deviated to one side, and if the patient is having respiratory distress, it may be a serious sign of a tension pneumothorax.

122. Subcutaneous emphysema: air under the skin from chest/lung trauma. May puff up, feel 'spongy' and is often related to serious injury and respiratory distress. Most likely found at the neck, chest, and upper back.

123. Paradoxical chest wall movement: related to a "flail chest" where several ribs are broken in several places creating a loose chest segment (floating segment) as that area moves in the opposite direction of the rest of the chest with each inspiration and expiration. Can be stabilized with direct hand pressure or pressure from a bulking dressing taped to the chest.

124. Sucking chest wound: penetrating trauma to the chest large enough to let air move in and out of the wound with each breath. Use *occlusive* (seals air and moisture) dressing taped on three sides to try to create a *flap valve* that seals on inspiration but lets air escape from the wound on expiration (to try to prevent a tension pneumothorax). If breathing gets worse after placing the dressing remove it. A sucking chest wound is better than a tension pneumothorax.

125. Guarding: a patient's protective reaction from the pain of palpation, often on the abdomen. They may tense up or pull away.

126. Pulsating mass: in the abdomen, may be related to a *dissecting aneurysm* (bulging of a weakness in an artery that may burst) and the feeling of the patient's pulse in that area. In the abdomen it will be on the aorta.

127. Priapism: a sustained erection in a male patient due to spinal trauma.

128. Incontinence: *loss of bowel or bladder control.* Common with seizure, fainting, stroke.

129. Fistula: in the arm, a surgical joining of an artery and vein to create a large vessel for easy IV access during dialysis (for *renal,* kidney, failure.) Be gentle with this area, don't take blood pressure on that arm or lift the patient putting pressure on the area.

130. Sacral edema: *a build-up of fluid in the tissues of the low back.* May be from prolonged bed rest without proper movement or repositioning.

131. The Golden Hour: from the time of an injury until the patient receives *definitive* treatment. *Definitive care* is care that fixes the injury, not just first aid. For shock or serious trauma, such care should be given in less than one hour for the best chance of recovery.

132. The Platinum 10: the goal to examine, treat, and begin transport of the patient within ten minutes of our arrival on scene.

133. Reassessment: reassess the patient every 15 minutes if stable, at least every 5 minutes if unstable.

134. Decompensated shock: the patient's vital signs may remain close to normal as the body *compensates* for blood loss, usually with a faster than normal pulse. The mechanism of the injury, possible signs of shock, and our impression of the patient is more important than normal vital signs when deciding on rapid transport. The patient's vital signs may change quickly as the patient *decompensates* and is unable to maintain a stable blood pressure. Especially true in children.

135. Patient history: The EMT will develop their own routine when gathering a patient history. The questions we ask will vary with the patient complaint. "Hi, what happened today?" or "What seems to be bothering you the most?" will allow the patient to relate important information. We observe and measure *signs* (such as *skin signs* and *vital signs*) and the patient relates *symptoms* (things they *feel* that we cannot observes or measure). We may need to ask questions of family members or bystanders if our patient cannot communicate fully with us.

136. Mechanism of injury: we need to fully understand the details of what happened in order to think of potential injuries and treatment and to paint the correct picture of the incident to the receiving doctor or nurse. If they fell off a ladder, how high on the ladder were they? Did they fall of grass or concrete or carpet? What made them fall? Did they miss a step? Did they get dizzy?

137. OPQRST: Probably most useful for *Chest Pain* but can be used on other complaints.

Onset (what were they doing when this happened) **Provoking factor** (does anything make this better or worse) **Quality** (what does this feel like, describe it to you) **Region/Radiation** (where exactly is it and does it go anywhere else) **Severity** (how bad is this on a scale of 1-10 with 10 being the worst they've ever felt) **Time** (how long has this been going on, has it been constant or has it come and gone.)

138. Pertinent negatives: Signs or symptoms the patient does NOT have that you might expect they would based on their complaint.

139. SAMPLE: Signs and **S**ymptoms, **A**llergies, **M**edications, **P**ertinent past medical history, **L**ast oral intake, **E**vents leading up to this complaint.

140. Auscultate: *to listen* to, such as lung sounds with a stethoscope.

141. Palpate: *to feel* or touch the patient for signs of illness or injury.

142. Blood pressure: taking a blood pressure is a routine skill for the EMT. The top number is the *Systolic* pressure (the main pumping pressure of the left ventricle) and the bottom number is the *Diastolic* pressure (the resting pressure within system as the heart refills with blood). Using a stethoscope to listen while taking a blood pressure is known as *auscultating a blood pressure*, not using a stethoscope and only feeling the pulse to get only a systolic blood pressure is known as *palpating a blood pressure* (when the on scene noise is too high to hear with a stethoscope).

143. The Secondary Assessment: After our *initial* or *primary assessment* and perhaps a *rapid assessment* for signs of trauma, we need to go back and do a more complete systematic assessment looking for other details. *(this was discussed in #118)*

144. The Focused Assessment: a more detailed evaluation of a specific complaint or specific injury.

145. Stridor: a high-pitched crowing sound that may indicate an upper airway obstruction in the mouth or throat, *physical* *obstruction* (from some foreign object) or *anatomical obstruction* (from some part of the person's body, such as swelling or injury).

146. Breathing and breath sounds: we assess for *rate, rhythm, effort*, and *tidal volume*. Normal rate is 12-20 breaths/min. for adults. The rhythm of normal breathing should be *regular* not *irregular*. The use of any *accessory muscles* to assist breathing is a sign of *respiratory distress*. **Tidal volume** is our estimation of whether the depth of the breaths (the amount of air moving in or out) is normal, too little, or greater than normal. Unusual breath sounds may include: **snoring** sounds (usually from the tongue or some object in the airway) **wheezing**, high-pitched whistling from a narrowing of the airways, **crackles/rales**, a wet crackling sound from fluid in the lungs, **rhonchi**, a low-pitched noisy sound from mucus and often with a productive cough.

147. Cardio-vascular: Normal pulse rate is 60-100 beats per minute. Over 100 beats is called a **Tachycardia** and less than 60 is a **Bradycardia**. The pulse should be *regular* and should not skip beats called an *irregular pulse*. We can check a pulse for 30 seconds and multiply times two to get the rate. If we feel an *irregular pulse*, we should check the rate for a full minute. An *irregular pulse* is usually a sign of a **cardiac arrythmia**. There are many types of cardiac arrythmias, and many are dangerous and can lead to weakness or fainting, cardiac arrest, heart attack, or stroke. A paramedic unit should generally be called to evaluate a patient with an irregular pulse. The *quality* of a pulse can be described at **bounding** for an unusually strong pulse or **thready** for a weak and hard to feel pulse.

148. Blood pressure: Blood pressure can drop due to a loss of blood, loss of *vessel tone* causing the vessels to open up (dilate) or from a problem with the heart causing it to pump inadequately. The patient may become dizzy, confused, or unconscious. As blood pressure drops the body may attempt to *compensate* by *increasing the heart rate* and *constricting the vessels*. Low blood pressure must be treated, or the lack of perfusion can be deadly. Infusion of fluids are often an initial treatment. High blood pressure can result from chronic artery disease and plaque in the vessels that narrows the vessels and causes the heart to beat harder through the obstructions. Too much pressure in the arteries of the brain can cause them to rupture causing a stroke.

149. Hypotension = low blood pressure. **Normal BP** = less than 120/80

150. Hypertension = high blood pressure. Higher than 140/90 (New AHA number for hypertension is **130/80**)

151. Neurologic system: We need to evaluate patients for proper functioning of the brain. **AVPU** (**A**lert, **V**erbal, **P**ain, **U**nresponsive) is a basic measure of a patient's *level of consciousness*; whether they are **alert** and responding normally, whether it takes a **verbal** stimulus to get them to respond, or if a **painful** stimulus is needed to make them respond, or whether they are **unresponsive** to all stimulus.

152. Pupils: The pupil in the center of the eye is an opening for light to get in and land on the *retina*. The size of the pupil changes as the muscle of the iris constricts or dilates from signals sent through the **oculomotor nerve** (the 3rd cranial nerve). The pupils are normally the same size. A small number of people have a harmless condition known as *anisocoria* that can cause unequal pupils. Except for that condition, the EMT will be very concerned if they find a patient with unequal pupils.

153. Pupil size and slow or no pupil response can indicate a serious problem: we are concerned that there may be an injury to the brain from trauma or a stroke, brain tumor, lack of oxygen, drugs or medications.

154. PMS - Pulse, Motor, Sensation: Checking the *distal* (ends) of the extremities (hands and feet) for PMS can confirm basic neurological functioning. **Pulse**, is it present and equal, is the skin color and temperature normal? **Motor**, can the patient wiggle fingers and toes. **Sensation**, can they feel your touch, and does it feel normal to them.

155. Pedal pulses: refers to pulses in the feet. The ***dorsalis pedis*** pulse is on the top and center of the foot. The ***posterior tibial*** pulse is behind the ankle bone on the medial (inside) aspect of the foot.

156. Pulse Oximetry: *measures the saturation of oxygen* in the hemoglobin of the blood. The device is usually attached to the patient's finger. It may give inaccurate readings if the patient is in shock or if they have carbon monoxide poisoning.

157. Capnography: devices that can measure CO2 in exhaled air, usually a device used by Paramedics.

158. Blood glucometry: devices that measure blood *glucose* (sugar). An EMT skill that involves a needle stick to a finger and using a glucose meter to determine blood sugar readings.

159. Airway management: Without oxygen the brain will begin to die in 4-6 minutes. ***Diffusion*** is the process that moves molecules <u>from an area of high concentration into an area of lower concentration</u>. *Diffusion* moves oxygen from the lungs across the membranes of the *alveoli* into the hemoglobin which is then carried by red blood cells into capillaries that oxygenate the cells and tissues. It is also diffusion that allows carbon dioxide produced by the cells to move into the air sacs where it is exhaled.

160. The Respiratory System: is made up of all the components that form the *airway* and are involved in our ability to breathe (ventilate.) ***Inhalation*** occurs then the *intercostal muscles* between the ribs pull the rib cage outward and the *diaphragm* contracts pulling the lungs downward. These movements create *negative pressure*, a *vacuum*, which draws air into the airways to the lungs. *Exhalation* is generally passive, as the rib cage relaxes, and air is exhaled. The **upper airway** is all the parts of the airway <u>above the vocal cords</u> (the nose, mouth, jaw, oral cavity, pharynx, larynx). The ***pharynx*** is the whole length of the throat, from the nose and mouth to the *esophagus* and *trachea*. The ***nasopharynx*** is the area of the nose, the ***oropharynx*** or oral cavity contains the hard and soft *palate*, the cheeks, and the tongue. Beyond the tongue the ***epiglottis*** has a fold or flap that covers the ***larynx*** when eating or drinking to prevent such contents from entering the trachea. *Aspiration* occurs when food or fluid enters the trachea, which can cause choking or even death.

161. The larynx: is where <u>the lower airway begins</u>. This structure contains the *vocal cords* and is made up of *thyroid cartilage* (the Adam's apple) the *cricothyroid membrane, cricoid cartilage*, and then the *trachea* begins.

162. Lower airway: delivers oxygen to the *alveoli*. The *trachea* begins just below the *cricoid cartilage* and down the neck to the *thoracic cavity*. In the thoracic cavity the trachea divides at the *carina* (the branch to the bronchi) into the right and left *bronchi* and into the *lungs* through smaller bronchi, *bronchioles*, and then to the balloon-like sacs of the *alveoli* which are surrounded by *capillaries* where oxygen enters the blood and carbon dioxide exits. A membrane called the **pleura** surrounds each lung. The pleura and the membrane of the thoracic cavity slip together reducing friction to allow easy movement of the lungs.

163. Intercostal muscles: are the muscles between the ribs which help expand the chest during inspiration. The **diaphragm** is the other major muscle of respiration that pulls the lungs down during inspiration to allow expansion of the lungs.

164. Mediastinum: *the space in the chest between the lungs* surrounded by tough tissue that *contains the heart, the great vessels, esophagus, trachea, bronchi, and many nerves.*

165. The phrenic nerve: in the thorax, controls the contraction of the diaphragm.

166. Blood flow: the right heart pumps *deoxygenated blood* to the lungs, the left heart pumps *oxygenated blood* to the body.

167. Patent: means *open*, as in a *patent airway* meaning an open unobstructed airway.

168. Hypoxia: the tissues and the cells don't get enough oxygen.

169. Hypoxic drive: the result of the late stages of COPD where the drive to breathe is controlled by *low levels of oxygen*. The *normal breathing drive* comes from *high levels of carbon dioxide* building up, stimulating the need to increase breathing. ***Dyspnea*** is the term for *shortness of breath*, often making it difficult for the patient to speak in full sentences and increasing the respiratory rate and tidal volume.

170. Metabolism: also known as *cellular respiration*, is the process where cells create energy using oxygen and sugar and product waste products such as water and carbon dioxide.

171. Room air: contains 21% oxygen and 78% nitrogen (inert).

172. Aerobic metabolism, anaerobic metabolism: *Aerobic* metabolism is the *normal cellular metabolism* and creates *Carbon Dioxide* as a waste. CO2 can be breathed out and neutralized with *bicarbonates* produced in the body. ***Anaerobic*** is *abnormal metabolism* due to a lack of oxygen, producing *lactic acid* as a waste. Lactic acid, is dangerous, is hard for the body to deal with and get rid of.

173. Chemoreceptors: These receptors monitor changes in blood chemistry; such things as levels of oxygen, carbon dioxide, and pH of the spinal fluid. Changes detected by chemoreceptors cause adjustments in the body to the rate and depth of breathing and brain actions in the medulla to decrease pH levels. *Chemoreceptors in the carotid arteries and in the aortic arch detect decreased oxygen and low pH levels.*

174. Hypercarbia: An *increase of carbon dioxide levels* in the blood.

175. Carbon monoxide: *Carbon monoxide* will bind with *hemoglobin* in the blood blocking oxygen from the hemoglobin. Carbon monoxide is a product of *incomplete combustion* and can build up from malfunctioning heaters or lack of venting of exhaust, or a fire and smoke within an enclosed space.

176. Circulatory issues will affect proper respiration: The obstruction of blood flow can happen for many reasons; hemo or pneumothorax, embolism, sucking chest wound, heart failure, cardiac tamponade, blood loss, etc. Any condition that decreases perfusion to the lungs and body will have a negative effect, and if not corrected, ultimately leading to shock and death.

177. Shock: *widespread lack of perfusion to the body.* Shock is essentially caused by two main mechanisms, ***hypovolemic shock*** where there is inadequate blood volume, from blood loss or loss of other fluid in the blood such as that caused by dehydration (lack of water or loss from vomiting or diarrhea.) *Hypovolemic shock* means there is not enough blood for the heart to pump to all parts of the body. The other main cause of shock is *vasodilatory* shock, from dilation (widening) of vessels, lowering the blood pressure and again not allowing the heart to pump to all parts of the body. In this form of shock there can be an adequate amount of blood in the body, but the blood pressure is too low to properly pump it. Shock leads to *anaerobic metabolism* and ultimately death.

178. Normal breathing: Rate between 12 and 20 breaths per minute. A 'regular' pattern inhalation and exhalation. Clear and equal lung sounds bilaterally. Equal rise and fall of the chest with an adequate amount of air entering with each breath (tidal volume).

179. Breathing rates: Adult 12-20. Children 15-30. Infants 25-50.

180. Labored breathing: Use this term to describe a patient who is struggling to breath, using "accessory muscles" of the neck (sternocleidomastoid), the chest muscles (pectoralis major) or abdominal muscles to assist their breathing.

181. Retractions: Especially in children, the skin pulling in with each breath around the ribs or above the clavicles. This indicates labored breathing. Children or infants may also "grunt" while breathing which is a serious sign of difficulty breathing.

182. Agonal breathing: In cardiac arrest a patient may sometimes appear to be breathing, but the few irregular gasping breaths may be reflex breathing called "agonal" breaths. For patients in cardiac arrest taking agonal breaths, treat them as if they are not breathing and supply assisted breaths.

183. Cheyne Stokes respirations: May be seen in stroke or head injury, causing irregular breaths with increasing then decreasing depth and rate followed by periods of *apnea* (no breathing).

184. Ataxic breathing: Irregular and ineffective breathing with no pattern. May be caused my head injury.

185. Kussmaul respirations: Often related to the *metabolic acidosis* of *hyperglycemia*, these are deep, rapid respirations and may also have an unusual odor of *Ketones* (fruity smell).

186. Pallor: Pale skin related to poor perfusion. Continued poor perfusion will result in *cyanosis* (bluish color) often starting at the lips or fingertips. As the patient gets worse, they may develop *mottling*, blotching of the skin.

187. Pulse oximetry: measures the percentage of hemoglobin in arterial blood. Normal is 98-100%. Less than 96% is usually considered hypoxemia. When measured at the fingertip the pulse oximetry reading indicates what the oxygen levels were about one minute ago. If the patient has vasoconstriction the reading may not be accurate. Depending on the manufacturer's instructions, the pulse oximeter can also be attached at the bridge of the nose or the ear lobe. Inaccurate reading can result from hypovolemia, vasoconstriction, dark nail polish, dirty fingers, and carbon monoxide poisoning.

188. Capnometry / capnography: These devices, usually ALS equipment, measure exhaled CO_2. If exhaled CO_2 levels are low, there is usually something wrong.

189. A "patent" airway: "Patent" means open. A clear and open airway takes priority over most other concerns. If we suspect a spinal injury, but the patient is not breathing, we will be careful if we must move them (using help and a "log roll" procedure if possible) but we must quickly insure a proper airway and adequate breathing. *The possible spinal injury is NOT as important as insuring they are breathing!*

190. Head tilt-Chin lift maneuver: Pushing down on the forehead with one hand while pulling up under the chin with the other will often open the airway, usually by moving the tongue upward. This maneuver is called the *Head tilt – Chin lift.* This procedure moves the neck, and should be avoided with a suspected spinal injury, unless no other options are available or effective.

191. Jaw-Thrust maneuver: When we suspect a neck/spinal injury we should avoid twisting the spine or tilting the head back. Leaving the head in a neutral position, and from above the patient, place the fingers of both hands under the angle of the lower jaw and lift upwards, while the thumbs of both hands position the lower jaw in a slightly open position. If the *jaw-thrust* was needed to open the airway you may need to continue to hold it in that position while treating the patient.

192. Cross-finger technique: to open the mouth. Use the tips of the index finger and the thumb on the patient's teeth, then push down and up with the fingertips to open the mouth. Avoid placing fingers into a patient's mouth, they may bite down.

193. Suctioning: *"Noisy breathing is obstructed breathing."* If the patient is gurgling, suction them! If there is no neck injury, turn their head to one side to suction. You'll most likely have a built-in suction unit in your ambulance. You will have some sort of portable suction, battery operated or a simple manual hand-held unit. The standard suction end pieces (catheters) are either **rigid** or **flexible**. *Rigid* suction tips may be called *tonsil tips* or *Yankauer tips. Flexible* catheters are called *French* or *whistle-tip.* The standard *rigid catheters* are usually best for most purposes, being stiff and easy to maneuver and having a larger bore (wide diameter) opening. **Maximum suctioning time**: 15 seconds for adults, 10 seconds for children, 5 seconds for infants. Don't suction deeper than you can see! If secretions keep forming but you need to ventilate the patient, alternate suctioning with 2 minutes of ventilations.

194. Oropharyngeal airway: Short, stiff airways inserted into the mouth help to keep the tongue from obstructing the airway and make it easier to suction the airway. Used only in unconscious patients, who do not have a gag reflex.

195. Nasopharyngeal airway: Flexible rubber airway, lubricated then inserted into the nose, usually on unconscious or altered patients who are unable to maintain an adequate airway. Generally, not used on patients with severe facial trauma where we suspect facial fractures (which could allow the airway to enter the brain!)

196. Recovery position: for patients without trauma, they can be rolled onto their side, then their top leg is bent to stabilize them in that position, and their arm or hand is placed under their head to keep the head in a neutral position.

197. Oxygen: Oxygen cylinders come in several sizes. "D" or "Jumbo D" are the standard portable sizes we carry. The "M" size tank is often used as the 'on board' oxygen tank mounted in the ambulance. Oxygen tanks are usually filled to a pressure 2000 psi. A 'pressure regulator' is used to reduce that pressure to about 40-70 psi, and then a 'flow meter' adjusts to allow use on patient oxygen masks or nasal cannulas. Oxygen won't explode or burn but it supports or enhances burning, making a small spark or flame burn larger. **Nonrebreathing face mask**: for *high-flow* oxygen delivery (10-15 L/min.), may also have an attached *reservoir bag* to increase the percentage of oxygen delivered. It is called a "nonrebreather" mask because their exhaled CO_2 is vented away, not allowing them to rebreathe it. **Nasal cannula**: prongs placed in the nostrils allows a *low flow* of oxygen (1-6 L/min.). *The following data could be a future test question but won't be something you calculate or particularly care about in the field.* **Nasal cannula** delivers 24-44% oxygen. **Nonrebreathing mask with reservoir** delivers up to 95% oxygen. **BVM with reservoir** delivers nearly 100% oxygen.

198. Patients with a tracheostomy hole/stoma: they don't get oxygen from their nose and mouth; you would put your oxygen mask over the opening in their neck.

199. *Assisted breathing* **and** *artificial ventilation***:** A patient who is breathing on their own but not adequately, may require us to assist their breathing. We can use a BVM to administer a full breath as they breath in and add one if they do not breathe at least every 5-6 seconds. When the chest rises that is usually enough, we don't need to *fully* squeeze the bag of all its air. Artificial ventilation is required for patients not breathing on their own, using a BVM to administer a breath every 5-6 seconds. *(One breath every 3-5 seconds for children and infants).*

200. *Mouth to mouth* **or** *mouth to mask* **breathing:** We don't do it. Although they make "mouth to mask" devices we should not see such equipment as EMT's. Such devices may be common in some lower levels of training.

201. Bag-Valve-Mask: Those in charge of EMS systems seem to enjoy changing the names of our procedures and our equipment. Currently, the BVM is in the process of becoming the BMD (Bag-Mask-Device). They are the same thing. *Most EMT textbooks talk of the BVM being a two-person device. Rarely will that be necessary.* A patient with a particularly injured face or jaw or a patient with dentures might require one EMT to seal the mask and another to squeeze the bag, but the BVM is commonly a one-person device. You should become expert at using it under difficult situations and while your patient is in unusual positions.

202. *Gastric distention* **from** *gastric inflation***:** Ventilating too forcefully or continuing to add air after the chest rises can cause too much pressure, allowing air to enter the stomach; this is caused gastric distention or gastric inflation. Excess air in the stomach can cause the patient to vomit.

203. FBAO: (Foreign Body Airway Obstruction) A *foreign body* is some *object* that doesn't belong in the airway, these obstructions must be removed manually or using a choking procedure such as

"The Heimlich Maneuver" or CPR. An *anatomical obstruction* is a part of the patient's body that causes an airway obstruction, the most common cause being the *tongue*. Swelling or damaged tissue from *trauma* is another *anatomical* cause as is narrowing airways from swelling caused by *allergic reactions*. We must obtain a rapid *history* of what happened to determine if an airway issue is from a *foreign body* or from some *medical cause* such as stroke, heart attack, seizure, drug overdose, or other cause.

MEDICATIONS*: Which medications the EMT may administer and the precise methods and dose can vary from state to state, even from county to county within a state.*

204. Pharmacology: *The science of drugs/medications.* Even *oxygen* is a medication. An ***indication*** is the reason why a particular medication is necessary. A ***contraindication*** is a reason why a particular drug should NOT be used. Routes of administration of medications: **sublingual** (under the tongue) **intravenous** (into a vein) **intraosseous** (a needle into a bone) **inhalation** (breathed in) **intranasal** (into the nose) **intramuscular** (through a needle into a muscle).

205. Metered-dose inhaler: such as an asthma inhaler, delivers a specific dose of medication with one squeeze of the inhaler.

206. Topical medication: cream or ointment. Effects surface of the skin only.

207. Transcutaneous/transdermal: medications *absorbed into the blood stream through the skin*. (Such as: Nitroglycerin, nicotine, birth control, pain medicines).

208. Gel: such as glucose paste for diabetics.

209. The "Six Rights" of Medication Administration: The right *patient*, right *medication*, right *dose*, right *route*, right *time*, right *documentation*.

210. EMT medications: Oxygen, Activated Charcoal, Oral glucose, Aspirin, Epinephrine, Metered-dose medications, Nitroglycerin, Naloxone. (Varies by local protocols).

211. Activated charcoal: charcoal powder that can bind with/absorb harmful substances/medications and prevent them from entering the blood stream. Usual dose: 1 to 2 g/kg (grams per kilogram) of body weight. *(Divide the patient's weight in pounds by 2.2 to determine their weight in kilograms).*

212. Aspirin: given *for chest pain* to reduce formation of blood clots. Dose: 160-325 mg. of chewable aspirin.

213. MDI (Metered-dose inhaler) *albuterol* (Proventil, Ventolin) for *vasoconstriction*, causes vasodilation. Dose: 1 to 2 inhalations.

214. Epinephrine (EpiPen): for *anaphylactic reaction*, causes bronchodilation. Dose: 0.3 mg for adults; 0.15 mg for children.

215. Naloxone (Narcan): For *opioid overdose*, reverses respiratory depression. Dose: 0.4 mg auto-injector; 2 mg IN/intranasal.

216. Nitroglycerin: For chest pain, dilates arteries. Dose: 0.3 to 04 mg SL/sublingual. 0.4 mg spray.

217. Oxygen: *May be harmful to patients having a heart attack or stroke if their breathing is normal and their oxygen saturation is 94% or higher!*

218. Shock: Trauma, as well as several medical conditions, can result in shock. Shock is: *Widespread inadequate perfusion*, or *hypoperfusion*. **Perfusion**: the circulation of blood to all the organs and tissues to provide oxygen, nutrients, and waste removal. In "shock" the body is failing to properly perfuse, and the body will react by trying to maintain proper *homeostasis* (balance of all body systems) by *compensating*, usually by raising the pulse rate, and constricting vessels to maintain the blood pressure. As shock progresses the body will be unable to maintain proper perfusion and the blood pressure will fall, ultimately causing death if not corrected.

219. The blood: *red blood cells* (carry oxygen to cells and carbon dioxide away from cells), *white blood cells* (fight infection), *platelets* (assist in blood clotting), and *plasma* (the liquid portion of the blood).

220. Blood pressure: *Systolic pressure* (the peak pressure every time the heart contracts and ejects blood from the left ventricle). *Diastolic pressure* (the resting pressure in the arteries as the heart is refilling and preparing to beat again). *Pulse pressure*: the difference between the systolic and diastolic pressure = the amount of force generated by each contraction of the heart.

221. Sphincters: *Circular muscles*. Capillary sphincters constrict and dilate to control blood flow to cells and organs. This controls various needs in the body brought on by changes in heat, cold, oxygen requirements, and the need for waste removal.

222. The Autonomic nervous system: (automatic) responding to *hormones*. The *sympathetic* responses are the *fight-or-flight* mechanisms from the release of hormones such as *epinephrine* and *norepinephrine* to increase heart rate and cardiac contractility and causes vasoconstriction of nonessential areas such as the skin and gut (gastrointestinal tract). The *parasympathetic* system controls involuntary functions by sending signals to glandular muscles as well as cardiac, and smooth muscles.

223. Shock: There are 3 ways shock can occur; the "pump" (heart) can fail from damage or malfunction or from a blockage that restricts its blood supply, inadequate blood volume, or issue that cause the vessels to dilate. In Los Angeles county the four specific 'types' of shock are called: *Cardiogenic, Obstructive, Hypovolemic*, and *Distributive*, which represent in order the causes of shock listed above. In *Cardiogenic* shock the heart (pump) itself is not working properly, heart attack and other heart or vessels diseases or trauma can cause this. In *Obstructive* shock something is blocking the blood flow, such as an embolism (pulmonary embolism) or other issue where the blood flow through a vessel is reduced such as from an *aneurysm*, or from *cardiac tamponade* or *tension pneumothorax*. **Hypovolemic** shock results from a reduced blood volume, from blood loss or the loss of other fluids that make up the blood volume, such as losing water from dehydration, vomiting, diarrhea, or even from burns. ***Distributive*** shock results when the blood pools or is *distributed* to area of the body other than where it is needed from unusual vessel dilation, which can be the result of infections, poisons, spinal injury, allergic reaction, even fright. The four shock categories listed above cover all the causes of shock, but many books teach other specific names for shock as the result of each specific cause such as; *Cardiogenic*, *Obstructive*, *Distributive*: (Septic, Neurogenic, Anaphylactic, Psychogenic) *Hypovolemic*: (Hemorrhagic, and Non-Hemorrhagic shock).

224. Preload: the pressure in the heart before a contraction occurs.

225. Afterload: the force that the heart pumps against.

226. Pulmonary edema: the buildup of fluid in the lungs.

227. Pericardia effusion: *fluid between the pericardial sac and the myocardium*. Can be from trauma, infection, cancer and other conditions. If this fluid continues to build up it can lead to **cardiac tamponade.** Fluid around the heart from *cardiac tamponade* can decrease filling of the heart and decrease cardiac output.

228. Beck's triad: the three major signs of *cardiac tamponade*: jugular vein distention, muffled heart sounds, and narrowing pulse pressure.

229. Tension pneumothorax: usually from an injury; *air escapes from the lung into the chest cavity* causing pressure that can collapse the lung and then compress against the heart and aorta. Can cause ***tracheal deviation*** (pushes the trachea off to one side) and *absent lung sounds* on the effected side.

230. Pulmonary embolism: *blood clot blocking blood flow in the pulmonary circulation.* Prevents blood from being pumped from the right side of the heart to the left side. *Pulmonary embolism* is more likely to occur after a recent surgery or fracture, after childbirth, from prolonged bed rest, or from other prolonging lack of movement such as sitting during a long airplane flight.

231. Syncope: *fainting*

232. *Compensated* or *decompensated* shock: In the **early stages** of shock the body will attempt to *compensate*, usually *by increasing the pulse to increase the blood pressure.* In the **late stages** of shock, the body can no longer effectively compensate, and *the blood pressure begins to fall.* If not treated the patient will die. Children and infants can often maintain their blood pressure until they have lost nearly half of their blood volume; once their blood pressure falls, they are often near death.

233. CPR: Our assessment of the scene and patient(s) should quickly determine if the scene is safe and we can approach the patient, if we need additional resources or equipment, if the patient has any obvious life threats such as active and serious bleeding, if are responsive, if they are breathing adequately, and if they have a pulse. If CPR is needed, we must begin immediately while calling for ALS assistance and applying the AED. **ROSC**: *Return Of Spontaneous Circulation* is our goal, but we must be prepared to administer CPR continuously during transport if the patient remains pulseless. *Even is done perfectly, CPR only supplies about 1/3 of the normal blood circulation, CPR alone won't save them.*

234. AED: *Automated External Defibrillator.* A patient in *cardiac arrest* (or *full arrest*, meaning no breathing and no pulse) is often in *ventricular fibrillation*, where the heart is simply quivering and not pumping. The AED can momentarily stop ALL electrical activity in the heart, erasing v-fib, in hopes that the heart is healthy enough to recharge and begin pumping again. ***To be most effective the patient in cardiac arrest must receive the AED shock(s) within the first few minutes of their cardiac arrest! Time is critical!***

235. Active Compression-Decompression CPR: CPR creates intrathoracic pressure which squeezes the heart causing blood to circulate. The lungs are also squeezed with each chest compression, causing air to move in and out of the lungs with each push of the chest. We must allow our hands to come up completely after each compression of the chest, leaving no downward pressure on the sternum, to ensure the greatest intrathoracic pressure and the most effective flow of blood. That is called *full chest recoil*, when we make sure there is NO pressure on the chest after each compression. With *Active Compression-Decompression devices* (basically a suction cup device that allows us to pull upward after the downward compression) we can generate even greater intrathoracic pressures and greater blood flow with CPR. *These devices are not widely used at this time.*

236. Cardiac arrest in children and infants: is usually caused from a respiratory problem leading to cardiac arrest; often a choking, accidental drug ingestion, drowning, electrocution, infection, injury, and SIDS. We should always be thinking "airway problem" when dealing with children or infants in cardiac arrest.

237. Rescue breathing: *breathing for the patient. Cardiac arrest* is also known as *full arrest*, meaning no breathing *and* no pulse. In *respiratory arrest* the patient does have a pulse but *is not breathing.* In this case they do not need chest compressions, only "rescue breathing." Give one breath every 3-5 seconds for children and infants, and one breath every 5-6 seconds for adults.

238. Obvious signs of death: We should not begin CPR on patients who meet criteria for being 'obviously dead.' These rules can vary, you should be familiar with your local protocols. *Signs of obvious death: Rigor mortis* (stiffening of the body), *Dependent lividity* (livor mortis) is a discoloration of the skin from blood pooling in the dependent parts, *Putrefaction* (decomposition), Obvious *non-survivable trauma* such as decapitation, dismemberment, massive burns, massive crush injury.

239. DNR, POLST, MOLST: Patients may have an official order informing you they do no want to be resuscitated, or that they have certain procedures they want and others they do not. *Most often these patients have some terminal illness.* **DNR** = *Do not resuscitate*, meaning you should not resuscitate their breathing or pulse, no artificial ventilations and no CPR. **POLST** = *Physician's Order for Life-Sustaining Treatment* or **MOLST** = *Medical Orders for Life-Sustaining Treatment*, which are doctor's orders detailing what procedures they can and cannot have.

240. Heimlich maneuver (Abdominal-Thrust Maneuver): The procedure for relieving a foreign-body in a responsive choking patient over 1-year-old. When unresponsive with a foreign-body obstruction we do CPR, checking the mouth for an object each time before attempting breaths. *Responsive infants with a foreign body choking, we do 5 back blows (back slaps) followed by 5 quick chest thrusts, repeated.*

241. Cardiac arrest and pregnancy: with full-term or close to full-term patients, the weight of the baby can compress the *aorta* and *vena cava* reducing blood flow to the heart and body. <u>During CPR you should use one or two hands at about the level of the umbilicus to significantly move the uterus to the left and maintain this during CPR</u>. *For other full- or near-term pregnant patients not in cardiac arrest, position them on their left side during transport.*

242. NOI – Nature of illness – *to determine the signs and symptoms to then determine the appropriate treatment for a specific complaint.*

243. MOI – Mechanism of injury – *to determine what happened, and how to treat a particular injury in light of what body part may be injured.*

244. Assessments: Begin with a *Scene Size-up*, then *Primary Assessment*, *History taking, Secondary Assessment*, and *Reassessment.*

245. Epidemic vs. Pandemic: An *epidemic* is an outbreak of a disease that is greater than expected, a *pandemic* is a worldwide breakout of a disease.

246. Influenza = *the flu*

247. HIV: is the virus that can lead to AIDS. Infection can come from sexual contact or contact with bodily fluids.

248. Bacteria: grow outside the body and can cause disease when they enter the body.

249. Virus: smaller than bacteria, grow inside a host body.

250. Fungi: like bacteria they grow outside the body, *mold* is an example.

251. Protozoa: one-celled amoebas.

252. Helminths (parasites): such as worms.

253. Hepatitis: inflammation / infection of the liver. May cause yellowish skin and eyes (jaundice) and right upper quadrant abdominal pain. *Hepatitis A comes from contaminated food. Hepatitis B and C are transmitted from contact with infected blood. Patients using IV drugs are at high risk of hepatitis B and C, and HIV.*

254. Meningitis: *inflammation/infection of the meninges* (the membranes covering the brain and spinal cord). Fever, headache, stiff neck, altered level of consciousness are signs. Most often caused by viruses or bacteria and not contagious, except for **meningococcal meningitis** which is *very* contagious and sometimes deadly *(these patients often have red blotches on their skin),* but red blotches alone can't determine if it is the contagious or non-contagious form. *Patients with meningitis may simply have flu-like symptoms and can spread the disease by coughing and sneezing.*

255. Tuberculosis: spread by coughing. *Patients with active and contagious TB will usually have a cough; other signs are fever, fatigue, night sweats, weight loss.*

256. Whooping cough: also known as *pertussis*. Airborne, usually affecting children less than 6 years old. Often make a 'whoop' sound when trying to inhale after an episode of coughing.

257. MRSA – *Methicillin-Resistant Staphylococcus Aureus.* **An infection highly resistant to antibiotics.** *Most often transmitted from unwashed hands of healthcare workers!*

258. History of recent overseas travel: Disease like *Ebola* from Africa, and *MERS-CoV* from the middle east and immigrants from other countries where vaccinations are not common present a health risk. If you encounter a patient who is ill and has a recent history of traveling to another country, use a HEPPA mask on them and you, ask where they have traveled, and if anyone else in their group is sick. This history is important so that the appropriate agency can be contacted if needed to prevent further spread of the disease.

259. Dyspnea: shortness of breath or difficulty breathing.

260. Hypoxic drive: related to chronic COPD conditions, where the patient's body relies on *low oxygen levels to trigger increased breathing* rather than our *normal breathing drive related to increasing levels of CO2 to trigger an increased need for breathing.* (Because the emphysema patient has constant higher levels of CO2, they no longer have the normal breathing drive that is triggered by increasing levels of CO2). Giving the COPD / Emphysema patient high levels of oxygen could cause respiratory depression because of this faulty hypoxic drive system, but **we should never withhold or limit oxygen to these patients**, simply use a BVM with oxygen to breath *for* the patient if their breathing slows down after giving oxygen.

261. Croup: A viral infection progressing into inflammation and swelling of the pharynx, larynx, and trachea. Causes a deep, barking, seal-like cough. Usually in children from 3 months to less than 3 years old. Is spread between children. Use *humidified oxygen* if available. Parents may have these children in an enclosed bathroom with a hot shower running to create steam;

which is a good treatment! Albuterol is *not* a treatment and may make things worse!

262. Epiglottitis: *life-threatening inflammation of the epiglottis.* Caused by a bacteria and usually found in infants and children. Causes a very sore throat, which causes the patient to sit forward in a *tripod position*, and they are often *drooling* to avoid painful swallowing. Limit your exam to avoid making them cry, which could cause a spasm and worsen the airway obstruction; give *blow-by* oxygen if a mask on their face might make them cry. *Prompt transport!*

263. Blow-by Oxygen: an oxygen mask held *near* the young patient's face to give some oxygen without the mask on their face, which could cause them to cry and worsen their SOB. Do not blow oxygen in the patient's eyes! *(Recommended for epiglottitis).*

264. RSV (Respiratory Syncytial Virus): common in children, can be spread in school environment, causes **infection in lungs and airways**. Highly contagious! Give humidified oxygen if available.

265. Pneumonia: *a general term for an infection in the lungs.*

266. Pulmonary edema: fluid in the alveoli of the lungs, may hear wet or crackling sound on auscultation (crackles, rales). A result of congestive heart failure, often with a history of high blood pressure, coronary artery disease, or atrial fibrillation. *Pulmonary edema is not always part of a cardiac history; poison, smoke inhalation, toxic fumes, chest trauma, and high altitudes can all cause pulmonary edema.*

267. COPD, Chronic Obstructive Pulmonary Disease: A general term representing **emphysema** and **chronic bronchitis**. The *emphysema* patient usually has *chronic bronchitis* as well, coughing up sputum, having a chronic cough, difficulty expelling air, long expiration phases and wheezing as well as crackles or rhonchi. These patients are often thin with barrel-chests (enlarged chests).

268. Asthma: an acute (sudden) *spasm of the bronchioles* along with excessive mucus production and swelling of the mucous lining of the airways. The patient usually has a long history and know what triggers their symptoms. Triggers can be certain foods or allergen, exercise, emotional stress, or respiratory infections. Usually treated with albuterol inhaler or nebulizer.

269. Anaphylaxis: *Severe allergic reaction* with airway swelling, hives (urticaria), itching, and shock. **Epinephrine** (EpiPen) is a common treatment along with *antihistamines* such as *Diphenhydramine* (Benadryl).

270. Pneumothorax: *a build up of air in the pleural space.* Usually from trauma, but a ***spontaneous pneumothorax*** can occur from some medical conditions that weaken the lung or from lung infections. **Pleuritic chest pain** is a sharp pain on one side of the chest that is made worse with respirations. If we suspected a possible heart attack, for example, but their pain was worse with breathing, we would suspect a lung issue as the more likely explanation. *Remember always that multiple issues may be occurring at the same time.*

271. Pleural Effusion: *a collection of fluid outside the lung on one or both sides of the chest,* often in response to any irritation, infection, including CHF (Congestive Heart Failure) and even cancer.

272. Embolus: *anything in the circulatory system that moves from one point to a more distant point and obstructs the flow of blood beyond that site.* An embolus can be a blood clot, a foreign body, or even an air bubble. *(An air bubble in the **arterial** system is a big threat, in the **venous** system a much lesser threat).*

273. Pulmonary embolism: *a blood clot from the legs, pelvis, or right atrium that lodges in the pulmonary artery and obstructs blood flow.* Life-threatening. Patients at greatest risk of pulmonary embolism; prolonged bed rest or prolonged lack of movement such as a long plane flight, recent fracture or surgery, recent pregnancy, even cancer.

274. Hyperventilation: *overbreathing to the point of causing a drop in arterial levels of carbon dioxide.* Can result from hyperglycemia, aspirin overdose (causing acidosis), severe infection, or an emotional upset. Breathing away too much CO2 can cause **alkalosis** which upsets the body's homeostasis (balance). *Hyperventilation syndrome* (also known as a panic attack) is from some *emotional upset*, causing shortness of breath, anxiety, dizziness, tingling and numbness in the hands and feet and sometimes causes **carpopedal spasms** (painful cramping of the hands and feet). If the patient calms down the effects will gradually go away. *Hyperventilation syndrome* from emotional upset is not dangerous to most people with no other serious medical conditions but **we do not know in the field if this is just an emotional upset or if other more serious reasons could be the cause.** Always treat them as if it is the most serious condition related to their signs and symptoms and allow the physician at the hospital to diagnose the actual cause.

275. HazMat = *Hazardous Materials.* Things such as pesticides, cleaning chemicals, ammonia, chlorine, gasoline, acids, gasses, or any substance potentially harmful should be considered a *HazMat* incident. Those with proper protective clothing and appropriate respiratory protection will handle these calls. If we determine a hazardous chemical or substance is present, we will usually withdraw to a safe area and call for a *HazMat* unit. A patient exposed to a hazardous material should be decontaminated properly before we handle them.

276. Carbon Monoxide poisoning: highly poisonous but odorless, colorless, and tasteless carbon monoxide is known as "the silent killer." It is the product of incomplete combustion and is often associated with malfunctioning indoor heaters in homes. Anything that burns with a flame and is not properly vented can produce carbon monoxide. Winter is a more dangerous time of year when people tend to have doors and windows closed and heaters running. Exposed patients may have flu-like symptoms, headache, confusion, nausea and vomiting, and may become unconscious, have seizures, and may die. If we suspect carbon monoxide poisoning in an enclosed area, move yourself and your patient outside quickly and call for HazMat.

277. Adventitious breath sounds = *abnormal breath sounds*, such as wheezing, crackles (rales), rhonchi, gurgling, snoring, and stridor.

278. Electrical Conduction System in the heart: Begins in the **SA** (Sinus node) in the upper part of the right atrium, travels across both atria causing them to contract, crosses the **AV** (atrioventricular node) slowing the signal down, then spreads across both ventricles through *the bundle of His* and through the *right and left bundle branches* and through the *Purkinje fibers* causing the ventricles to contract.

279. Ischemia: *lack of blood flow to an area*, in the heart a lack of blood flow causing ischemia will result in chest pain or chest discomfort. If ischemic tissue is deprived of blood flow long enough it will die, or *infarct*. A *myocardial infarct*, or M.I. is death of some heart tissue.

280. Atherosclerosis: (hardening of arteries) *is a buildup of calcium and cholesterol (fatty material) which forms a plaque inside the walls of vessels*, obstructing blood flow and reducing the ability of the vessels to dilate or contract. **CAD** (coronary artery disease) when plaque forms in the coronary vessels is a leading cause of heart attack.

281. Dependent edema: buildup of fluid in the tissues of the feet and legs (most dependent parts). One of the signs related to **CHF**. If the right side of the heart is damaged, fluid collects in the body.

282. Hypertension (high blood pressure): *blood pressures with either number over 140/90 is considered hypertension*. A *hypertensive emergency* exists with systolic pressures over 180; such patients are at severe risk of *stroke* or *dissecting aortic aneurysm*.

283. Aortic aneurysm: *weakness (bulging) in the wall of the aorta.* "Dissecting" aneurysm means the inner layers of the aorta are separated allowing blood to flow between them. Signs/symptoms: Sudden severe 'tearing' pain in the chest or between the shoulders in the back; may have unequal blood pressures in the arms and diminished pulses in the feet.

284. Code 3 transport or not? *Not all patients need Code 3 transport to the hospital.* For patients with minor complaints and stable vital signs we should usually NOT go Code 3. Even for a patient with *abnormal* vital signs and serious complaints we should think of the *Risk vs. Benefit of Code 3 transport.* As an example; a patient with clear signs of a stroke or heart attack needs to get to the hospital right away, that is clear. But we should measure how much time will be saved going Code 3, which is usually NOT significant on most transports, vs. the further potential negative effects of a Code 3, lights and sirens, transport. Code 3 transport is bound to raise the anxiety of our patient, which is likely to increase their pulse rate and their blood pressure. Can we harm a stroke patient by raising their blood pressure? Yes. Can we harm a patient having a heart attack by increasing their pulse and the oxygen demands on the heart? Yes. Also, patients with "ugly" and/or "significant" injuries such as large lacerations or fractures may not benefit from Code 3 transport. When we save two minutes racing a patient with a nasty cut or fracture to the hospital and then discover the definitive care for the injury won't occur for perhaps and hour or more at the hospital, we should question such Code 3 transports. We are much more likely to be involved in a traffic accident when driving Code 3. *Remember, not all patients need Code 3 transport to the hospital, think of the Risk vs. Benefit of Code 3 transport!*

285. Nitroglycerin: *for chest pain or chest discomfort.* Dilates vessels bringing increased oxygen supply to the coronary arteries. Given sublingual (under the tongue) in pill form or a spray. Patient's blood pressure must be over 100 systolic. We must wait at least 5 minutes before giving another if we give a dose or if they have already taken a dose; rechecking the blood pressure before another dose. We cannot exceed their prescribed dose. They cannot have used an erectile dysfunction medication within 24 hours.

They may get dizzy or get a headache or have a fall in blood pressure from the nitroglycerin.

286. EKG (ECG): Electrocardiogram. (The 'K' in EKG is from the German spelling). The 12-lead ECG/EKG is the norm in most places, usually an ALS/Paramedic skill, requiring some study to learn the specific placement of The 3-lead EKG is simple, with the white lead near the right arm/shoulder/clavicle, the black lead across from that on the left side, the red lead below the black lead under the left rib cage, and the green lead across from that under the right rib cage. *(White goes on the right, smoke (black) above fire (red)* is one way to remember the locations.

287. Pacemakers and **implanted defibrillators:** under the skin, usually on the left upper chest, the size of a silver dollar. Pacemakers create an electrical impulse to cause a heartbeat, may be set to beat continually or only when needed to assist the heart. Implanted defibrillators can deliver a shock, like an AED, to get rid of ventricular fibrillation. The shock is not strong externally and poses no risk to rescuers. Treat patients with these implanted devices as any other patient if they are in cardiac arrest, using CPR and your AED when indicated. Place your AED patches, if needed, *just below* implanted devices if they are in the area the patch should go. Other devices such as **LVADs** *(left ventricular assist devices)* are pumps to assist the heart and may be implanted but with an external battery. *Local protocols should provide guidance if the EMT has any role in the care or operation of such devices.*

288. Using an AED: Patches that go on the chest have pictures showing proper placement. Defibrillation with the AED should be done rapidly within seconds of arriving on scene and finding a patient in cardiac arrest. (Only use the AED on patients with NO PULSE and NO BREATHING and NO SIGNS OF LIFE). Do not let anyone touch the patient when delivering a shock; hands up and away and shout "Clear!" before pushing the shock button. Restart CPR immediately after the shock is delivered or if the machine says, "No shock advised." The AED will only shock *Ventricular Fibrillation* and *pulseless Ventricular Tachycardia.* Move patients out of water, dry the chest of wet patients, remove medication patches from the chest and wipe the area with a towel. Shave excessively hairy chests where patches will be placed. Every two minutes the AED will tell you to stop CPR as it reanalyzes the heart rhythm; the rescuers doing CPR switch places every time the AED stops to reanalyze. Do not use the AED in a moving vehicle. When transporting, leave the chest patches in place but turn the AED off.

289. Neurologic emergencies: Brain disorders and disease such as Stroke, Seizure, Tumor, Trauma, Intoxication, Metabolic problems.

290. Three major parts of the brain: brain stem, cerebellum, cerebrum. **Brain stem**: controls basic functions such as breathing, blood pressure, swallowing, and pupils. **Cerebellum**: just behind the brain stem, responsible for muscle and body coordination of complex tasks. **Cerebrum**: above the cerebellum, divided into right and left hemispheres, each hemisphere controls actions on the opposite side of the body. The front of the cerebrum controls emotion and thinking, the middle part sensation and movement, and the back part controls sight. Speech is controlled by the left side near the middle. Twelve *cranial nerves* go from the brain to various parts of the head; eyes, ears, nose, face. Other nerves exit the brain with the spinal cord through the hole at the base of the skull, the *foramen magnum*.

291. Headaches: the brain and bony skull do not have pain receptors. Pain from a headache comes from either the face, scalp, meninges (membrane around the brain and spinal cord) blood vessels, or muscles of the head, neck, or face. *Migraine headaches* are probably caused by changes in the size of blood vessels near the base of the brain and can be severe and associated with nausea, vomiting, or vision disturbances, and may last for several hours or even days. *Sinus headaches* result from pressure build up from fluid in the sinus cavities. These patients may have cold or flu-like symptoms, nasal congestion, cough, or fever. *To the EMT a headache is a big deal*; thinking of the worse case scenario we should consider possible stroke, tumor, meningitis, trauma, poisoning, or overdose. *Remember that our patients with what may seem like a minor complaint, such as a headache, have called 9-1-1 because this was unusual and frightening to them and should be taken seriously by EMS.*

292. Signs of stroke: headache, slurred speech (dysarthria), facial drooping, one-sided weakness or paralysis = hemiparesis (weakness) or hemiparalysis, loss of balance, trouble swallowing, confusion, combativeness; *aphasia* (inability to speak), *expressive aphasia* (inability to use the right words), *receptive aphasia* (difficulty understanding speech). Part of *The Cincinnati Prehospital Stroke Scale* is to ask the possible stroke patient to repeat this sentence: **"The sky is blue in Cincinnati."** If they cannot repeat or slur the words that is an important sign of possible stroke. *Arm drift:* with their eyes closed, have the patient hold out both arms in front of them with their palms facing up for 10 seconds. If one arm drifts down that is a possible sign of stroke. Routine use of oxygen NOT recommended in stroke patient with no respiratory distress. Maintain Spo2 of 94%.

293. TIA (Transient Ischemic Attack): signs and symptoms of a stroke that go away on their own in 24 hours or less. 1/3 of TIA patients go on to have a stroke. May be from a small clot that resolves on its own.

294. Postictal state: may mimic a stroke, this is the *sleepy or confused period after a seizure*, usually lasts from 5 to 30 minutes.

295. Subdural or **epidural bleed:** from head trauma, a *subdural bleed* may bleed slowly and may take many hours or days to develop. An *epidural bleed* occurs rapidly. Any confusion or loss of consciousness after head trauma puts the patient at risk of bleeding on the brain.

296. Seizure (epilepsy): A patient with a history of seizure activity is considered an *epileptic*. Seizures can come from trauma, congenital illness, drug use/overdose, alcohol withdrawal, hypoglycemia, hypoxia, metabolic problems, and tumors. The common picture of a seizure is the *grand-mal seizure*, where the patient has full-body shaking (tonic-clonic) movement and loses consciousness; usually followed by a short ***post-ictal period*** of confusion, sleepiness, or combativeness. The patient is often ***incontinent*** (incontinence), losing control of their bladder or bowel. Seizures can take many forms, with only some part of the body shaking, the patients remaining awake during a partial seizure. Many seizure patients experience an ***aura***, a sensation of some sound or colors or smells letting them know a seizure is about to occur.

Note: Many seizure patients with a long history of epilepsy will become alert and refuse transport. We should always advise them to be evaluated by a doctor. We will be less worried and might agree with their refusal if:

- The patient is now awake and fully oriented
- No trauma is involved.
- They have a long history of seizures.
- This seizure was the same sort of seizure they have frequently.
- The patient is on appropriate medication and sees their physician regularly.

297. Status epilepticus: although patients with a long history of seizures may accept their seizures as part of their lives, under some conditions seizure activity becomes more life-threatening. ***Status epilepticus*** is defined as repeated seizures without becoming conscious between them, more than 3 seizures in an hour, or seizures lasting longer than 30 minutes. Paramedics may be able to control seizure activity with medication. It may be difficult to use positive pressure breathing (BVM) during a seizure due to spasms of the chest and diaphragm.

298. Febrile seizure: *caused by fever*, most common in children.

299. Syncope: *fainting (having a **syncopal episode** = fainting)*

300. Altered mental status: *being confused/not fully alert.* The **AEIOU-TIPS** pneumonic is useful to determine possible causes. You may need a friend or family member to determine this history. **A**lcohol, **E**pilepsy, **I**nsulin (diabetic), **O**piates/**O**verdose, **U**remia (kidney failure), **T**rauma/**T**emperature, **I**nfection, **P**oisoning/**P**sychiatric causes, **S**hock/**S**moke.

301. Glasgow Coma Scale (GCS): For patients with any altered mental status. Evaluates *eye opening*, *verbal response*, and *motor response* with points given for the response in each category. *15 is a perfect score.* Maximum points: Eyes **4**, Verbal **5**, Motor **6**.

Eye opening: spontaneous 4, responds to *speech* 3, responds to *pain* 2, no response 1.
Verbal response: oriented 5, confused 4, *inappropriate* words 3, *incomprehensible* sounds 2, no response 1.
Motor response: *obeys* commands 6, *localizes* pain 5, *withdraws* to pain 4, abnormal *flexion* 3, abnormal *extension* 2, no response 1.

302. Gastrointestinal and **Urologic emergencies:** The *abdominal cavity* is divided at the *umbilicus* into **four quadrants**. There are *solid organs*; *liver, spleen, pancreas, kidneys,* and *ovaries*. The kidneys, ovaries, and pancreas are behind the membrane surrounding the other abdominal organs (the **peritoneum**) and are therefore considered *retroperitoneal*. Solid organs are more likely to cause bleeding and shock when damaged from bleeding. *Hollow organs*; *gallbladder, stomach, small* and *large intestines, bladder*. These organs can cause abdominal pain when injured or diseased, often leaking contents into the abdominal cavity. An **acute abdomen** is a term to describe a sudden onset of abdominal pain from medial conditions or trauma. An inflammation of the abdominal lining, the *peritoneum*, is called *peritonitis*. Inflammation of small pockets of the intestine is called *diverticulitis*. **Cholecystitis** is an inflammation of the *gallbladder*. **Appendicitis** is an inflammation/infection of the *appendix* usually accompanied by fever and often right lower abdominal pain. Inflammation of the *peritoneum* can cause pain at a distant point in the body not related to other organs that might be involved, this is called *referred pain*. Gallbladder issues (*cholecystitis*) can cause *referred pain to the right shoulder.* An **ulcer** is an erosion of the lining of the stomach or intestines and can lead to bleeding. Such patients often complain of heartburn, nausea, vomiting, belching/gas. Often occurs after eating. **GERD** *(gastroesophageal reflux disease)* is related to a malfunction of the sphincter between the esophagus and the stomach, allowing stomach acid into the esophagus. **Hematemesis** is vomiting blood. **Melena** is black, tarry stools from digested blood. **Coffee ground emesis**, flakey black or brown material from partially digested blood. **Gallstones**, forming a blockage in the gallbladder and leading to *cholecystitis*. Often related to eating fatty foods. **Pancreatitis**, inflammation of the *pancreas* can be caused by an obstructing gallstone. Severe pain both upper quadrants often radiates to the back. **Esophageal varices** is an enlargement of vessels in the *esophagus* often from liver failure; often related to alcohol abuse. If esophageal vessels rupture the patient may vomit life-threatening amounts of blood. **Hemorrhoids** are *enlarged vessels near the anus/rectum*. May occur from pressure during pregnancy and straining or bearing down while having a bowel movement. Bleeding will be bright red in the toilet. **UTI** = *Urinary Tract Infection*. **Kidneys** (known as the *renal* system) filter wastes from the blood, a malfunction can lead to **uremia**, as the waste product *urea* builds up. **Kidney stones** are crystallized chemicals that may build up and block a *ureter* (urine tubule) causing pain. Sometimes a *kidney stone* will pass (be peed out) on its own, sometimes other treatment or surgery is required. If the kidneys are damaged (renal failure) and can no longer function a kidney transplant or regular *dialysis* (connecting to a machine to filter the blood) will be required. An *abdominal aortic aneurysm* (**AAA**) is a weakness or bulging of the *aorta* which can rupture. Causes severe tearing pain that may radiate to the back. Can present with a *pulsating mass* in the abdomen. **Hernia** is a protrusion of an organ though a hole into an area it doesn't belong, often from a weakness in the tissue. An *inguinal hernia*, in the groin, may allow a portion of intestine to move into the *scrotum* of a male, causing enlargement. The patient may be able to push on the area and push the portion of the protrusion back in where it belongs, which is called a *reducible* hernia, but it will later return. This may be a long-term condition and may not need immediate surgery to repair unless it is no longer *reducible.*

303. Pertinent negatives: You assessment of patients will include the finding of *pertinent negatives*, which are things you might suspect in a given situation but the patient does not have, such as reporting that the patient *denies shortness or breath* or radiation of pain, or there was *no loss of consciousness.*

304. Endocrine system: A system of glands that secrete hormones which travel to cells, tissues, and organs causing certain affects.

305. Glucose and oxygen: are necessary for cells and organs to function. The **pancreas** produces two *hormones* that control *glucose metabolism*; *glucagon* and *insulin*. An area of the pancreas is known as **the islets of Langerhans**, which are areas containing *alpha* and *beta* cells; the **alpha cells produce glucagon** and the **beta cells produce insulin**. **Diabetes mellitus** (diabetes) is a disorder of this glucose metabolism where proper levels of glucose cannot reach the cells.

306. Diabetes: Type 1 (Juvenile onset), **Type 2** (Adult onset). In *Type 1* diabetes the body cannot produce insulin and these patients must inject insulin every day to survive. *Type 2* diabetes is related to issues that stress the pancreas, such as obesity; these patients most often take oral medication along with limits on their diets. *Diabetics* are prone to dangerous swings in their *blood sugar levels*, causing either *low blood sugar* (**Hypoglycemia**) or *high blood sugar* (**Hyperglycemia**.) Diabetes effects all tissues of the body, particularly the kidneys, eyes, small arteries, and peripheral nerves. We will often see long-term diabetics with related issues such as heart disease, vision problems, renal failure, stroke, and infections of the feet or toes.

307. Patients with diabetes, especially *Type 1 diabetes*, have issues related to eating and drinking and effects on the kidneys that cause issues with thirst and urine production. **Polyuria**, *frequent urination*. **Polydipsia**, *excessive thirst*. **Polyphagia**, *increased hunger*.

308. Ketones: dangerous chemical acids formed when there is not enough insulin and the body begins to use fat for energy. This results in an abnormal *acid-base balance* in the body and may cause *Kussmaul respirations*, fast, deep breathing *(and a fruity, sweet smelling breath)* as the body tries to reduce acid levels by breathing out more CO_2. As this progresses the body may enter a life-threatening situation called **diabetic ketoacidosis (DKA)**. Patients often have abdominal pain, nausea, vomiting, and ultimately an altered level of consciousness. Their blood sugar levels will be high (**hyperglycemia**).

309. Hypoglycemia: *low blood sugar levels*. Causes: a change in eating or exercise routines *(such as taking their insulin or medication but not eating, or vigorous exercise that uses up more insulin than normal),* too much insulin will quickly deplete the available glucose, and illness can put greater demands on the bodies insulin/glucose balance. *__Hyperglycemia__ often occurs quickly* when insulin levels change whereas *__hypoglycemia__ usually takes longer to cause problems.* The patient with hypoglycemia is often confused, dizzy, combative, sweaty, and may faint or have a seizure or become unconscious.

310. Oral glucose: as *a treatment for hypoglycemia*, usually in a tube, this glucose paste is given in the mouth onto the mucous membranes and is quickly absorbed. Local protocols will dictate exactly how you will administer it.

311. Sickle cell disease: more common in people of African, Caribbean, and South American ancestry. Misshapen (sickle shaped) red blood cells create problems with oxygen binding and sudden clot formation causing anemia, gallstones, jaundice, spleen dysfunction, sudden ischemia of tissues, stroke, joint pain, eye problems, and increased risk of infection.

312. Hemophilia: a rare disease that causes excessive bleeding even with minor wounds.

313. Deep Vein Thrombosis: (**DVT**) common in patients who are sedentary (lack of movement) even truck drivers, long distance airplane travelers, and following injury or surgery, especially joint replacement. The main threat is that the clot will travel from the lower extremities to the lungs causing a **pulmonary embolus**, resulting in shortness or breath, chest pain, and even cardiac arrest.

314. The immune system: *protects the body from foreign substances and organisms* by triggering responses to inactivate the foreign agent. These responses can trigger an **allergic reaction**

from *histamines* being released. An *allergen*, that triggers this reaction, can be almost anything; medication, plants, dust, bits and stings, pollen, or a certain food item. We can become *sensitized* to a substance, such as a bee sting, but have little reaction to it. But the next time we are exposed to that same substance it might trigger a *serious allergic reaction*, or **anaphylaxis**, causing itching, redness, hives (urticaria), swelling, shortness of breath/wheezing. With *anaphylaxis* we are most worried about swelling that involves the *airways*, which can result in a life-threatening airway obstruction. A cough, or wheeze, or any trouble breathing following an allergic reaction should prompt our rapid transport.

315. Stings: bees have barbed stingers that cannot be pulled out by the bee, causing a part of the bee's abdomen to tear away after it stings and flies away, killing the bee. *(We should remove the bee stinger immediately if possible; if part of the bee's abdomen is still attached it can continue to inject venom).* Wasps and hornets don't have that issue and can sting repeatedly.

316. Wheal: the term for the whitish, raised area of the skin that often occurs from an insect bit or sting.

317. Epinephrine (EpiPen): a *sympathomimetic hormone* mimicking the sympathetic *fight or flight response*. For *anaphylaxis*, it constricts blood vessels to reverse vasodilation and resulting hypotension. Increases cardiac contractility and relieves bronchospasm in the lungs.

318. Toxicology: a *poison* is any substance whose chemical action can damage or impair the body. A *toxin* is a poison produced by animals, plants, or bacteria that changes or destroys cells. If you feel it is safe to do so, place possible poisons the patient may have been exposed to in a plastic bag and bring it to the hospital with the patient, this includes medications or empty pill bottles or other containers to help the doctor determine how best to treat the patient. Consider calling dispatch for a **HazMat** unit if a hazardous substance remains at the scene. The *four ways a poison can enter the body*; **ingestion**, **inhalation**, **injection**, **absorption**. (I.I.I.A.) An EMT can contact *The Poison Control Center*, 24 hours a day, to see if a substance is dangerous or needs further follow-up with a physician. 1-800-222-1222

319. MSDS (Material Safety Data Sheet) or **SDA (Safety Data Sheet)** should be available at any industrial facility where potentially hazardous substances are used. Ask for the MSDS for the chemical in question for more information on handling the patient and to give to the personnel at the hospital. If you believe the scene or patient is contaminated and may be dangerous to you, stay back and wait for *HazMat* to decontaminate the patient. <u>Never transport a contaminated patient into the hospital facility</u>, notify *HazMat* and the receiving hospital, the patient may need to be initially treated *outside* of the receiving facility.

320. Activated charcoal: can absorb some poisons and reduce the exposure/absorption to the patient. Not recommended for ingested alkali poisons, ethanol, methanol, cyanide, iron, lithium, mineral acids, or organic solvents, or in patients with a diminished level of consciousness. *The normal dose* is 1 g per kilogram of body weight (about 30-100 g for adults) (about 15-30 g for children less than 13 years old). *Follow local protocols.*

321. Alcohol: *the EMT should never minimize a patient who appears intoxicated with alcohol as simply "drunk."* Alcohol is a powerful CNS (Central Nervous System) **depressant**, a **sedative** that decreases activity and excitement, and a **hypnotic** that induces sleep. Many alcohol intoxicated patients have other drugs or medications in their system. These patients almost always have some decreased level of consciousness or confusion which could be a sign of alcohol poisoning, injury, stroke, drug overdose, diabetic emergency, or other medical problem. *They should be transported to the hospital for evaluation.*

322. Delirium tremens (DT's): can occur 1-7 days after stopping or significantly reducing the use of alcohol. Can cause sight and sound hallucinations, agitation, fever, sweating, shaking (tremors), confusion, and even seizures which can be life-threatening.

323. Opioids: a narcotic derived from the opium poppy such as codeine and morphine, or produced synthetically such as meperidine, hydromorphone, oxycodone, hydrocodone, and methadone. *Pinpoint pupils* *are a sign of use*, and the major complication is *respiratory depression* leading to death. **Naloxone** (*Narcan*) is an antidote that reverses the effects of an opioid overdose. *Narcan* is often administered *intranasally* (in the nose) by EMTs but can be given IV or IM.

324. Sedatives-Hypnotic drugs: Barbiturates and benzodiazepines are common sedatives. The effects will be similar to alcohol, causing drowsiness. *Chloral hydrate* is one of these drugs and has been called a "knock-out" drug or "Mickey Finn." The "date rape" drug *Rohypnol* or "roofies" and *ketamine* or "Special K" are sometimes used in drinks to disable and confuse a person before a rape occurs. Intoxicated persons are at risk of airway obstruction from a relaxed tongue, vomiting and aspiration, respiratory depression, and even cardiac arrest.

325. Abused inhalants: causing similar CNS depression as is seen in sedatives and hypnotic drugs, these substances, such as acetone, toluene, Xylene, and hexane are found in cleaning compounds, glues, paint thinner, and lacquer. Gasoline may be used, or propellants used in spray cans of *freon* or other aerosol sprays. They are often poured or sprayed into a bag and breathed in, called "huffing." Oxygen is displaced by these substances causing brief euphoria. Damage to the brain is common with the repeated use of any of these substances. *These substances can make the patient* *hypersensitive to their own adrenaline*, *making them susceptible to ventricular fibrillation with any excitement or exertion. They should not even be allowed to walk to the ambulance to avoid any exertion.*

326. Sympathomimetics: stimulants ("uppers") such as *amphetamines* and *methamphetamine* (meth or "ice") **MDMA** (ecstasy, molly, Eve) **PCP** (angel dust), **Cocaine**, all causing hypertension, tachycardia, and excited state, and dilated pupils. *These patients are often very paranoid, may hallucinate, have seizure, and often have cardiac dysrhythmias or cardiac arrest.*

327. Bath salts: similar to MDMA in action. These are <u>not</u> actual 'bath salts' used in baths such as Epsom salt (magnesium sulfate), these drugs quite different and very dangerous. *Signs/symptoms*: *teeth-grinding, muscle twitching, lip-smacking, confusion, paranoia, hallucinations, headache,* and *tachycardia.*

328. Hallucinogens: cause hallucinations, seeing and/or hearing things that aren't there or alter sensory perception. LSD, PCP are classic hallucinogens. *The patient may be calm and suddenly become violent, use caution.* Transport <u>without</u> extra stimulus such as lights and sirens if possible, dim interior lights.

329. Anticholinergic agent: these medications or substances *block the parasympathetic nerves* and may be used as an *antidepressant.* An overdose may result in hyperthermia, dilated pupils, dry reddened skin and dry mucous membranes, and severe agitation. <u>Examples</u>: Atropine, diphenhydramine (Benadryl), Amitriptyline (Elavil), or Jimsonweed.

330. Cholinergic agents: cause overstimulation of body functions controlled by the parasympathetic nervous system. May be in the form of a *nerve agent* (poison gas) such as **sarin** or in *organophosphate insecticides*. Causes excess salivation, drooling, runny nose, urination, tearing of the eyes, and diarrhea. The mnemonics **DUMBELS** or **SLUDGEM** can be used to remember the signs and symptoms:

DUMBELS: **D**iarrhea, **U**rination, **M**iosis (constriction of pupils) and **M**uscle weakness, **B**radycardia/**B**ronchospasm/**B**ronchorrhea (discharge of mucus from the lungs), **E**mesis (vomiting), **L**acrimation (excessive tearing of eyes), **S**eizures/**S**alivation/**S**weating.

SLUDGEM: **S**alivation/**S**weating, **L**acrimation, **U**rination, **D**efecation/**D**rooling/**D**iarrhea, **G**astric upset and cramps, **E**mesis, **M**uscle twitching and **M**iosis.

The agents/chemicals can cling to clothing and skin and require *HazMat* intervention before handling.

331. DuoDote: you might have access to a treatment for exposure to a *nerve agent*; the *DuoDote auto-injector* contains 2 mg of **atropine** and 600 mg of **pralidoxime**. If exposed inject YOURSELF with it. *Follow local protocols.*

332. Acetaminophen (Tylenol) overdose: A fatal dose is possible if an infant or child is given an adult dose! Tylenol overdose must be treated quickly at the hospital to avoid severe liver damage or death.

333. Ethylene glycol (antifreeze): Dangerous and deadly, sometimes used in suicide or murder attempts.

334. Salmonella is a bacterium that can be in food and can cause poisoning resulting in nausea, vomiting, abdominal pain, diarrhea, fever, and weakness. **Staphylococcus** can grow on left-over food with symptoms (nausea, vomiting, diarrhea) usually in 2-3 hours, sometimes 8-12 hours, after ingestion. **Botulism** (often from improperly canned food) is often fatal, caused my spores of *Clostridium bacteria*. Symptoms can be within 24 hours or up to 4 days with neurologic symptoms such as blurred vision, trouble speaking, trouble breathing, muscle paralysis. *The EMT won't know the exact cause of such illness, but knowledge of these problems will help to take seriously a simple complaint like a sudden bout of nausea or vomiting or stomach cramps. We should **always think of the worst-case scenario and treat the patient as if they may have that.***

335. Poisonous plants: we always err on the side of caution, and transport patients to the hospital who are in distress or may have come in contact with something potentially harmful.

Some poisonous plants: Dieffenbachia, Mistletoe, Castor Bean, Nightshade, Foxglove, Rhododendron, Jimsonweed, Death camas, Poison Ivy, Poison Oak, Pokeweed, Rosary pea, Poison sumac.

You aren't expected to be a botanist, or to memorize a long list of poisonous plants, but you never know what the National Registry EMT exam might ask about!

336. Psychiatric emergencies: Mental illness is something EMTs will deal with frequently. Such patients are often in the midst of a *behavioral crisis,* perhaps posing a threat to themselves or to others, which causes friends, family, or the public to call us, and often the police, to help control or treat them. One main concern is that such patients may become violent. Keep these patients away from potential weapons, such as kitchen knives, and be prepared to defend yourself and/or exit quickly if needed. The police should usually be involved in these calls. Such psychiatric emergencies can be the result of emotional stress, drugs or alcohol, psychiatric diseases, head trauma, or medical conditions such as diabetes, stroke, or electrolyte imbalances. Because of the potential for violence, stay calm and reassure the patient you are there to help, take your time to gather a history and understand the patient's specific story, avoid getting too close, and be clear about your treatment and transport plans. Your partner might gather history from a family member while you speak with the patient. *Always try to have help, EMS, fire, or police, in the back of the ambulance when treating and transporting these patients in case they become unruly.*

337. Restraints: follow your local protocols. Generally, patients can be restrained if they pose a danger to themselves or to others. EMTs most often use "soft restraints" (padded restraints) that don't easily injure the patient if they fight against them. You are allowed to use "reasonable" force to place the patient in restraints. Although law enforcement may restrain a suspect in handcuffs, hobbles on their feet, and perhaps "hog tied" with their hands secured to their restrained feet (hands and feet behind their back) often in a prone (face-down) position, EMTs should NEVER transport a patient in such restraints. *Positional asphyxia* can occur making breathing difficult and these patients may suffer respiratory or cardiac difficulties leading to death.

338. PTSD (Post Traumatic Stress Disorder): often caused by memories of traumatic events. Symptoms may include feeling helpless, angry, anxious, fearful, paranoid, hostile, depressed, guilty, and even shame. Combat veterans may have complications contributing to **PTSD** to include **TBI** (Traumatic Brain Injury) usually from explosions. We "should" ask if the patient feels suicidal. With patients that pose a *risk to themselves or others* we must insure we transport such patients, even if we must summon the police to place the patient on a "5150 hold" to insure they get help.

339. Gynecological emergencies: PID (Pelvic Inflammatory Disease) infection of female reproductive organs; *uterus, ovaries, fallopian tubes*. Generalized lower abdominal pain, vaginal discharge, weakness, fever, chills, nausea, vomiting. **Vaginal bleeding**; from trauma, ectopic pregnancy, miscarriage (spontaneous abortion), cervical polyps, cancer. **Rape/Sexual assault**: limit exam to emergency care of injury/bleeding, avoid questioning about the specifics of the attack, avoid disturbing evidence, discourage the patient from showering or cleaning up which could destroy evidence. **Perineum**: the skin between the vagina and the anus.

340. Trauma: *injuries caused by force.*

341. Index of suspicion: *our concern for unseen or underlying injuries* (always suspecting the **worst-case scenario**). We want o "raise" our *index of suspicion* to treat the patient as if they may have the worst not the least injury.

342. MOI (Mechanism of Injury): specifically, what caused the injury.

343. Newton's Laws: (Isaac Newton)

    First law: *An object at rest tend to stay at rest, objects in motion tend to stay in motion unless acted upon by some force. (A car traveling 40 miles an hour suddenly stops, the passengers continue forward at 40 miles an hour until they hit something.)*

    Second law: F=MxA *(Force equals mass times acceleration). Acceleration = is the change in velocity (speed) over time. Using that formula, the force on the body can be determined. If a car traveling 40 miles an hour slows down gradually the force* on the passengers is little. *If that car stops suddenly (hits a brick wall) the force will be great.*

Third law: *for every action there is an equal and opposite reaction. A patient whose body has impacted and bent the steering wheel makes you suspect that that force could likely have caused an injury to the patient as well.*

344. Multisystem trauma: a great force such as a long fall, high speed traffic accident, gunshot wound all make us suspect that *multiple body systems might be involved* (injured). Our *high index of suspicion* will make us suspicious of other hidden injuries even if all we can see at the moment is some isolated cuts or fractures.

345. Blunt trauma: *a force against the body that does not penetrate into the body.*

346. Penetrating trauma: *trauma that causes a piercing into the body; into organs, soft tissue, or body cavities.*

347. Coup-contrecoup injury: *in the skull, when the head forcibly hits something, and the brain continues to move forward striking the inside of the skull.* Results in bruising and/or tearing of the brain.

348. Car crashes: The EMT must inspect the vehicle the patient was in for signs that they may have struck the windshield, steering wheel, or other structures of the vehicle. ***Passenger space intrusion*** is the term for some part of the vehicle being pushed by the impact of the collision into an area the patient may have been in at the time of the crash. Descriptions of relevant vehicle damage and the nature of the collision should be relayed to the receiving staff at the hospital. We must *"paint a picture of the scene"* to the hospital with our written and verbal reports.

349. Deceleration injuries: *describes injuries caused by a rapid slowing of the body* in a crash or fall. In a car, the seatbelts and airbags are designed to more gently cushion the patient during *deceleration.*

350. Seat belt and airbag injuries: a seat belt's contact points on the body may cause injury to the patient and should be examined. *Air bags* often cause some injury to the face or chest and powders and explosives used in the airbags may result in respiratory issues from inhalation and/or burns.

351. Bullets: it may help the doctor to know what caliber or type of bullet was used, gather that info if available. More importantly, get the patient with a gunshot wound "**trauma naked**" *(most patients with serious trauma, regardless of the cause, where there may be hidden injury should have clothing removed, especially where small bullet holes may be hidden ALL the patient's clothing should be removed).* There may be an **exit wound** if there is an **entrance wound**, look carefully! *(Under arm pits, in folds of skin, etc.)* A bullet can travel a significant distance from where it entered. *Cavitation* is the term for the *internal injury/cavity* caused by the explosive pressure of the bullet.

352. Blast injuries: *Primary blast injuries*, injuries from extreme pressures close to the blast. *Secondary blast injuries*, injuries from flying bomb parts or other debris. *Tertiary blast injuries*, injuries from being thrown against something from the blast. *Quaternary blast injuries*, burns from hot gasses or fires, inhalation of smoke and toxins, suffocation, poisoning, crush injuries from building collapse, etc. The ear drum (*tympanic membrane*) is sensitive to injury from the pressures of an explosion; as are the *hollow organs* of the body, these pressure can also cause *pulmonary blast injuries* to the lungs, and *arterial air embolism*, causing neurologic injury, may also occur related to *pulmonary blast injury.*

353. The Golden Hour (*The Golden Period*)**:** A term to remind us that *definitive care* (the treatment that repairs or directly treats the underlying problem) should occur in *less than one hour from the time of injury.* The clock is ticking, by the time we arrive on scene it is common that ten minutes or more of that *Golden Hour* has already passed. Our *time on scene should be short* with serious trauma, our *transport should occur quickly*; remembering that *Golden Hour* and that ticking clock. *We should realize that most* *of our questioning of the patient, and much of our exam, can occur while we are in route to the hospital!*

The term **The Platinum Ten**, refers to our goal of ON-SCENE TIMES OF LESS THAN TEN MINTES for critically injured patients. There are times you will carefully **"Scoop-and-run"** the critical trauma patient, *transporting them after just a minute or two of quick exam and treatment*, with your other care done in route to the hospital!

354. Types of transport: Transport by ambulance, BLS or ALS, or perhaps by helicopter, the destination *(Trauma Center, Pediatric Hospital, Stroke Center, Heart Center, Burn Center, etc.)* and whether Code 3 or just driving, will be determined by the condition of the patient, your local resources, and your local protocols.

355. Trauma Centers: *Level 1 Trauma Center*, usually located at a University based teaching hospital, offers the best resources and capabilities to rapidly treat life-threatening trauma. *Level II Trauma Center*, often in a less-populated area does not have all the capabilities of a *Level 1 Center* but has special staff and equipment to enhance their ability to treat serious trauma. Your area may have other lower designations for lesser equipped trauma care facilities.

356. Hypoperfusion: inadequate perfusion of oxygenated blood to the organs and cells; results in *shock*. In an adult, blood loss of more than 20% or about 1 liter will cause shock. Children may compensate well for blood loss then *suddenly* go into shock.

357. Cardiovascular system: *the heart and the vessels; arteries, veins, capillaries.*

358. Hemostatic agent: *a chemical to improve clotting to stop bleeding.* May be infused into a dressing or may be a power or granules sprinkled on the wound.

359. Tourniquet: if we cannot quickly control serious bleeding on an extremity with *direct pressure* or a *pressure dressing* or *hemostatic agent*, we should consider placing a *tourniquet*. A commercial tourniquet, improvised tourniquet, or blood pressure cuff can be used. Place it a couple of inches above the wound. Once in place do not remove it. Note the time it was put on. *Transport quickly for further care.*

360. Epistaxis (nosebleed): from trauma, high blood pressure, dry air, sinus inflammation, intranasal drug use. Slight dripping should stop by itself and may need no intervention. The patient should lean forward slightly and be advised to spit out, not swallow, any blood; which often causes vomiting later. Significant bleeding from the nose can usually be controlled my 'firmly' pinching the fleshy upper part of the nostrils together and holding continually while you transport to the hospital. Don't let the patient blow their nose or force air out of their nose, which can increase the bleeding.

361. Bleeding from the ears: *cover with a loose dressing.* Completely blocking the blood flow could cause pressure to build up on the brain! If you see **"target sign"** (a blood spot surrounded by a large circle of clear fluid) suspect that **CSF**, *Cerebral Spinal Fluid* may be mixed with the blood, indicating a tear in the **meninges** (Dura, Arachnoid, and Pia layers) surrounding the brain and spinal cord.

362. Soft tissue injury: cut, scrape, or internal injury. Caused by blunt trauma (closed injury) or penetrating trauma (open injury), pressure injury (such as explosion or diving accident) or burns. Bleeding and later infection are important risks.

363. Skin: *epidermis*, the *tough external layer protective layer* of the skin. **Dermis**, contains *hair follicles*, *sweat glands*, *sebaceous glands* (produce *sebum*, an oily substance that waterproofs the skin), also *nerves*, *vessels*.

364. Mucous membranes: lining the mouth, eyelids, nose, anus, and vagina; similar to skin but secreting a watery lubricant to keep them moist.

365. Types of wounds: Contusion = bruise: from small blood vessel damage in the dermis. The blue or black color is called *ecchymosis*. **Abrasion** = a superficial *scrape* of the skin. **Laceration** = *a jagged cut* or tear in the skin. **Incision** = *a smooth-edged cut* from a sharp object. **Avulsion** = *a tearing away of a portion of skin causing a flap* of tissue or may be completely detached. *(If possible, replace the flap of skin in its proper position before bandaging, if detached transport the tissue as you would treat an amputated part).* **Amputation** = *a completely severed (cut off) body part.* Generally, put a *moist dressing* on exposed tissue of amputated part, put in *plastic bag*, and *keep cool* but do not freeze. *Transport such parts with the patient or have the part brought to the hospital as soon as possible if it must be found or extricated.*

366. Hematoma: a larger vessel is damaged, causing a buildup of blood under the skin usually forming a *lump*.

367. Crush injury: force causing tissue damage with continued compression of the area decreasing blood flow and causing more damage. *Toxins can be released after the pressure is removed, sometimes causing immediate unconsciousness or even death (see Crush Syndrome below).*

368. Crush syndrome: *from an area of the body trapped and compressed;* after *hours* of compression the damaged tissue and muscle cells die and release dangerous toxins. When the compression is relieved those toxins rush into the blood stream where they could quickly cause cardiac arrest and other organ damage. *Before the object that is crushing or compressing the patient is removed*, ALS should start and IV and may be able to administer treatment to lessen the dangerous effects of the released toxins.

369. Impaled objects: *an object stuck into the body.* Generally, do not remove impaled objects, unless you MUST remove them to do CPR or breathe for the patient or in order to transport them if they are impaled on something large. *(The impaled object may be able to be cut off rather than pulling the patient off it.)* Stabilize the impaled object if possible, to prevent it from moving, with bulky dressings, tape, and occlusive dressings near the wound if the injury is in the neck, chest, back, or upper abdomen.

370. Penetrating wounds to the neck, chest, back, upper abdomen: cover with an *occlusive dressing* to keep air from entering. *Occlusive dressings* form a *seal* to keep air and fluid in or out of an area; can be a piece of plastic, a *Vaseline* impregnated gauze, or other commercial occlusive dressing.

371. Fractures: *a broken bone.* Sometimes it is obvious when the bone is *protruding*, or a *severe angulation* is obvious, that a fracture has occurred. Often, with pain, swelling, or even deformity we may not know if we are dealing with a *fracture or a dislocation.* Treat areas of pain and swelling and/or deformity as if it is a fracture and apply a splint.

372. Evisceration: *an organ protruding from a body cavity through an open wound.* Do not push on the organ, cover with a moist saline dressing and then with an occlusive dressing and transport.

373. Neck injury: a cut to a large *vein* can suck in air, causing an *air embolism.* Significant neck injuries should be covered with an *occlusive dressing.* Consider there may be a possible head injury or spinal injury.

374. Animal bites: pose a significant risk of infection. Ensure your own safety and do not enter the area of an unsecured animal.

375. Human bites: pose a risk of infection as bad or worse than an animal bite.

376. Burns: consider a possible inhalation of smoke. Do not allow the patient or family to apply ointment to the burned area. Burn victims are at risk of infection, hypothermia, hypovolemia, and shock. Burns involving 'critical areas' (the face, airways, hands or feet, genitals or any burn completely around an area of the body (*circumferential burns*) are considered more serious. Burns on children should raise our suspicion of possible abuse. *Full-*

thickness burns (third-degree) involve all layers of the skin and may involve muscle, bone, or organs. The actual burned area may be *painless* due to destruction of nerves, although damage to surrounding skin may be painful second-degree burns. **Partial-thickness** burns (second-degree) involve the epidermis and some of the dermis and will form blisters. **Superficial burns** involve the epidermis, such as a *sunburn*.

377. The Rule of Nines: *a way to estimate the percentage of surface area burned.* **Adult**: (anterior or posterior) Head = 9%, Chest = 18, Back = 18, Arm = 9, Leg = 18. **Children** differences are in the head (12) and legs (16.5). **Infant** differences are head 18, legs 13.5.

378. Burn classifications: "**Severe**" any full-thickness burn, or a partial-thickness burn more than 20%. "**Moderate**" a partial thickness burn of 10-20%. "**Minor**" a partial thickness burn of less than 10%.

379. Types of burns: *Thermal (from heat), Electrical, Chemical, Radiation.* Causes: flame, scald (hot liquid), contact (touching hot object), steam, flash (sudden flare up or explosion of flame), inhalation (hot gases, often toxic gasses).

380. Chemical burns: with powdered chemicals, the dry chemical should be brushed off before flushing with water. Avoid inhalation by you or the patient of airborne powder. Other chemicals, flush with copious (large amount) of water. Chemicals in eyes should be flushed continuously in route to the hospital.

381. Radiation: *Alpha, Beta,* and *Gamma* particles. *Alpha* is blocked by the skin, *Beta* most is blocked by clothing, but *Gamma* can penetrate most things and is very dangerous.

382. Dressings: a *dressing* goes against the wound to protect and/or moisten the tissue; a **bandage** is some way of securing the dressing to the wound. *Sterile* dressings are preferred but a *clean* cloth or other material can be used if other dressings are not available or don't cover the wound, such as using a sheet to cover a large area of burned tissue.

383. The Head and Face: the *cranium* is made up of the *skull* and the *face*. The back of the skull is called the *occipital area*, the *temporal area* is on the sides around both ears, each side of the skull at the top are the *parietal areas*, and the very top of the skull is called the *vertex*. The forehead is called the *frontal skull*. The bony area forming the eye socket is the *orbit*. The external part of the ear is called the *pinna*. The *tragus* is a small rounded portion of the ear in front of the ear canal. The *mastoid process* is the bony area just under the ear.

384. The neck: the *Adam's apple* is a protruding area of *thyroid cartilage* marking the upper part of the *larynx* (voice box.) Below the *larynx* are rings of *cartilage* around the *trachea*. The *trachea* connects the opening of the mouth (the oral pharynx) to the *bronchioles* going to each lung. The ***sternocleidomastoid muscles*** are the major muscles on each side of the neck next to the *carotid arteries*; these muscles control movement of the head and can be signs of *respiratory distress* as the patient strains to breathe. **C7** is the last *cervical vertebrae* and can be palpated easily when the head is *flexed* forward.

385. The Eye: the *eyeball* is also known as the *globe* of the eye and contains jelly-like fluid called ***vitreous humor***. With an eye injury that could involve injury to the *globe* we should avoid applying pressure which might force out *vitreous humor* and further damage the eye. The inner surface of each eyelid is covered by a moist membrane called the *conjunctiva*. Tear glands, *lacrimal glands,* keep the eye moist. The white portion of the eye that forms the main structure of the globe is called the ***sclera***. At the front of the eye the ***cornea*** allows light to enter the eye. Behind the cornea lies the ***iris***, the colored circular muscle that contracts and dilates to adjust the amount of light entering the eye. The opening formed by the *iris* is the ***pupil***. The pupils normally appear the same size, but a condition that some people are born with called ***anisocoria*** is not uncommon and results in different sized pupils. Normally pupils that are not the same size are a concern for the EMT and may indicate a brain or eye injury. The **lens** of the eye is behind the *iris* and is the main structure to focus light. (The *cornea* also helps to focus light.) At the very back of the eye the **retina** has nerve endings that change light into nerve impulses that then travel through the **optic nerve** to the *brain* and are interpreted as *vision*. Trauma can cause a **detached retina** that could lead to blindness. Vision off to the sides while looking forward is called **peripheral vision.** *Use water or saline to flush particles or chemicals from eyes.* Eye lid can be *rolled back* with a Q-Tip to expose the inside of eye lid. Face can be placed into large basin and patient can blink and move eyes to flush, or under a faucet with running water. Take care not to contaminate the unaffected eye if flushing a chemical.

386. Injuries to the face, neck, head: we always worry about potential injury to the *cervical spine* (neck) with an injury to the head. The patient's airway may be compromised from injury to the nose, mouth, or boney structures of the face forming the *sinuses*. Damaged teeth can cause airway obstruction, as can swelling in the mouth and throat.

387. Broken or knocked out teeth: leave teeth alone if they are still partially attached. Save teeth and place in milk or sterile saline. Don't touch the 'root' of the tooth!

388. Subcutaneous emphysema: *air under the skin from trauma in the neck, chest, or back.*

389. Central nervous system: the brain and spinal cord. The brain is divided into the cerebrum, cerebellum, and the brainstem. Cerebrum controls most voluntary functions and conscious thought. The cerebellum control balance and coordination. The brainstem controls the most basic functions of heartbeat, breathing, and nerve transmission.

390. The peripheral nervous system: *sends nerve impulses to and from the spinal cord.* There are **31** pairs of *spinal nerves* and **12** pairs of *cranial nerves.* There are two parts of the nervous system, *the* **somatic** *nervous system controls* voluntary *functions, the* **autonomic** *nervous system controls* involuntary *functions.*

391. The skull: *four* major bones make up the *skull*. The *face* has **14** bones.

392. The spinal column: has **33** vertebrae, divided into five sections; the *cervical (7), thoracic (12), lumbar (5), sacral (5), coccygeal* (coccyx) *4*. Between each vertebra is a cushioning *intervertebral disk.*

393. Racoon eyes: *bruising under the eyes*, often indicates a skull fracture.

394. Battle sign: *bruising behind the ear* over the mastoid process, often indicates a skull fracture.

395. Basilar skull fracture: *a fracture at the base of the skull*, often from *high energy trauma* (motor vehicle accidents, falls.) May cause CSF draining from the ears from a ruptured *tympanic membrane*, increasing the risk of *bacterial meningitis* infection. Often accompanied by *Raccoon eyes* or *Battle sign*, which may occur quickly or take up to 24 hours to appear.

396. Traumatic brain injury (TBI): any significant trauma to the brain that may produce physical, intellectual, emotion or social, or vocational changes.

397. Cerebral edema (swelling of the brain): an injured brain swells from *cerebral vasodilation* and increased cerebral water build up (cerebral edema.) Low oxygen levels can increase cerebral edema. (Give high-flow oxygen.) These patients may have *seizure* activity. Swelling of the brain causes *pressure* (**intracranial pressure – ICP**) that can damage brain tissue, cause unusual breathing patterns, such as *Cheyne-Stokes* respirations, ataxic breathing. Other *signs of **increased pressure in the brain*** are, *decreased pulse, headache, nausea/vomiting, bradycardia, sluggish pupil response, decerebrate or decorticate posturing, and widening pulse pressure.*

398. Cushing's triad: the three signs that often indicate increased ICP (intercranial pressure): *increased systolic pressure, decreased pulse rate, irregular respirations.*

399. Epidural hematoma: *rapid <u>arterial</u> bleeding between the skull and dura layer*, usually the result of head trauma causing a fracture of the *temporal bone*. The patient is usually knocked unconscious, briefly regains consciousness (lucid interval) then goes back into unconsciousness and will die without rapid surgical intervention.

400. Subdural hematoma: <u>*venous*</u> *bleeding accumulating under the dura layer but outside of the brain*. Most often does NOT involve a skull fracture. From falls or *rapid deceleration* force. Occurs *gradually*, with periods of *confusion* and *slurred speech*.

401. Concussion: a short-lived period of confusion, "seeing stars," ringing in the ears, dizziness, lack of coordination, nausea and vomiting, and sometimes being briefly knocked-out, from a blow to the head. A concussion leaves no permanent damage but may cause a loss of memory of the event, *retrograde amnesia*. These patients may be alert and oriented by the time you arrive, but we should be concerned and transport any patient who had head trauma followed by confusion or unconsciousness.

402. Chest injuries: The chest or *thoracic cage* is that area from the lower end of the neck to the diaphragm. An injury of the spinal cord below C5 may cause the intercostal muscles to stop working but the patient should still be able to use their diaphragm to breath and cause noticeable "belly breathing." Spinal injury at C3 or above will stop all ability to breathe.

403. Traumatic asphyxia: *a sudden severe compression of the chest causing increased pressures*; causing distended neck veins, face, neck, and upper chest cyanosis, eye hemorrhage into the sclera. Such severe trauma is likely to cause damage to the heart and lungs or other organs.

404. Myocardial contusion: *bruising to the heart from blunt trauma to the chest.* May cause irregular pulse and dangerous arrhythmias as well as blood pressure changes.

405. Commotio Cordis: *a blunt injury directly over the heart that can cause instant ventricular fibrillation.* (From baseballs, softballs, kicks, or other sports trauma.) Should respond to rapid *defibrillation.*

406. Seat belt and airbag injuries are common: ask patient about seatbelt use, check shoulders, clavicles, abdomen for seatbelt trauma.

407. The "flank" *is the area on the patient's sides below the rib cage and above the hip; suspect injury to the kidneys with trauma in this area.*

408. Orthopedic injuries: *Tibia* (shinbone). *Fibula* (smaller leg bone). *Calcaneus* (heel bone). *Ligaments* hold joints together. Four mechanisms of injury: **direct force** and **indirect force** and **twisting forces** and **high-energy injuries**. *(Example of direct and indirect force: In a vehicle accident the patient's knee may strike the dashboard, a **direct force** injury, but the femur may also be injured from the **indirect force** transmitted to it.* An **open fracture** has the bone exposed through a cut in the skin, or it *was* exposed and may have been drawn back in. A **closed fracture**, the skin is not broken.

409. Nondisplaced & displaced fractures: *Nondisplaced,* also known as a *hairline fracture,* is a crack in a bone. A *displaced fracture* causes deformity, angulation, or a rotation or shortening of the limb.

410. Comminuted fracture: bone is broken into *more than two fragments.*

411. Greenstick fracture: *incomplete fracture,* may still cause a deformity; common in children.

412. Pathologic fracture: caused from *weakened or diseased bone*, such as *osteoporosis*; may not require much force to cause a fracture.

413. Spiral fracture: from a twisting or spinning force.

414. Crepitus: grating or grinding sensation felt or heard when bone ends rub together.

415. Ecchymosis: (bruising) almost always present at the fracture site.

416. A "locked joint" the patient cannot bend a joint; do not attempt to move the limb, may indicate a fracture.

417. Dislocation: a joint where *the bone ends are no longer in contact* and cannot move. Sometimes a *dislocated joint* may spontaneously *reduce* or *go back in the socket*. We should NOT try to *reduce* a dislocation unless you have special training and approval to do so.

418. Sprain: stress on a joint causing *stretching or tearing of ligaments*. Treat as a fracture. Patient may hear *pop* or *crack* sound.

419. Strain: *stretching or tearing of a muscle or tendon*. Patient may hear a *snap*.

420. Splinting: generally, we can use gentle *inline traction* while splinting to straighten a *severely angulated* extremity. If we meet resistance while applying *inline traction* leave the extremity in the position you found it and bend your splint to fit.

421. Before and after splinting: always check **PMS**, *Pulse*, *Motor* (movement), and *Sensation* before you manipulate the fractured area to splint, and after splinting is complete.

422. Traction splints: generally, for closed, mid-shaft, femur fractures with no other leg/pelvis injuries.

423. Pelvic binders: devices that can strap around a possibly fractured pelvis to stabilize it.

424. Acromioclavicular (AC) joint: at the end of the *clavicle* and the *acromion process* of the *scapula*, often separated from sports 'collision' injuries. Use a *sling & swathe* to stabilize.

425. Sling: can be used to around the lower arm to support its weight when treating an injury to the *humerus*, *shoulder*, and *clavicle*. The **swathe** is a cloth or bandage wrapped around sling and the body to hold the sling in close to prevent movement.

426. Hip fracture: *(a fracture of the neck of the femur)* the leg is often shortened and externally (outwardly/laterally) rotated.

427. Hip dislocation: *the leg is flexed and turned inward.*

428. Dislocation of the Patella (the *kneecap*): Often a sports injury, the *patella* is pushed off to the side (laterally).

429. Sprain and Strain treatment: splint as if fractured. **RICES** is a mnemonic for common treatment of sprains and strains and fractures; **R**est, **I**ce, **C**ompression, **E**levation, **S**plinting.

430. Compartment syndrome: *a buildup of pressure from bleeding, more common with 'crush injury'* but not uncommon with fractures of the *tibia* or *forearm*; pain out of proportion with the injury after 6-12 hours, pain on stretching of muscles, pale skin (pallor), decreased sensation and strength and movement. Prompt surgical intervention is needed.

431. Heat and Cold emergencies: Heat loss, or gain, occurs in several specific ways; through contact of a body part with a cold object, **Conduction**. Through the air, **Convection**. **Evaporation**. The **Radiation** of energy into the environment, or through **Respiration**.

432. Hypothermia: *a generalized lowering of the body temperature* that falls below 95 degrees F. Blood vessels constrict, shivering may begin, lips and fingertips may become blue (cyanotic), confusion occurs. Remove wet clothing, cover in blankets, give humidified oxygen if available, warm the ambulance compartment. Check pulse for 60 seconds before CPR, since bradycardia is common. *"No one is dead unless they are warm and dead"* is a saying to remind us to continue CPR at least until the patient is properly rewarmed.

433. Frostnip: *a freezing of the skin*, often ears, nose, fingers. Usually painless. Skin is pale. Does not extend into deeper tissues.

434. Frostbite: *a serious freezing of tissue causing permanent damage.* Over time dead cells will cause *necrosis* (gangrene) and the dead tissue will need to be amputated.

435. Hyperthermia: *heat gain exceeds heat loss*, and body core **temperature is 101 degrees F or higher**. *The three types of heat emergencies* are: **heat cramps**, **heat exhaustion**, **heat stroke**. Populations at greatest risk are the young, the old, patients with heart or lung conditions, diabetics, the obese and those with limited mobility, and those who are dehydrated.

436. Heat cramps: painful muscle spasms, usually after exertion. From sweating, dehydration, and changes in electrolyte balance.

437. Heat exhaustion: *(The most common heat emergency)* Often from overheating during exercise, often while wearing clothing that prevents evaporation of perspiration, or when people are unable to get out of a hot situation such as parades or large events. Weakness, dizziness, fatigue, syncope (fainting). Thirst, cold, clammy, pale skin.

438. Heat stroke: the most serious and life-threatening heat emergency. *The body's cooling mechanisms are overwhelmed, core body temperature may reach 106 degrees F or more.* Patient has hot dry skin, unconscious or very altered. Cool with ice packs in groin and armpits, and/or use moist towels or water spray and fanning. *Immersion in an ice bath* is mentioned in some texts, but *initially* such massive cooling could cause an *increase* in core body temperature due to massive vasoconstriction and may not be advised.

439. Drowning: *respiratory impairment from immersion in liquid.* *Near-drowning* is sometimes defined as a patient who survives for at least 24 hours after suffocation in liquid. Inhalation of water often causes a **laryngospasm,** *where the muscles of the larynx and vocal cords spasm and close.* After a drowning *laryngospasm* may make it difficult to ventilate the patient. In most drowning we should *suspect possible spinal injury* and take spinal motion restriction precautions. *Rescuers should have special training in proper water rescue techniques; the drowning person will often hold onto and push down the rescuer, sometimes drowning them! We should always use some flotation device or ladder or rope or other method to safely rescue someone in water.*

440. The *diving reflex* **or 'mammalian diving reflex'** *is the rapid slowing of the heart (bradycardia) when the body is suddenly immersed in very cold water.* This could cause someone diving into a cold lake, as an example, to become unconscious. The survival rate from drowning in very cold water is greater due to the protective effects of cold on the brain.

441. Decent and **ascent emergencies:** *Decent,* going down, most often seen in a *scuba diving* accident but can occur when *skin diving,* even in relatively shallow water. Usually *related to pressure building up as the depth increases,* causing lung, sinus, and ear problems. *Ascent* **emergencies** *are caused by rapidly returning to the surface,* usually after a deep dive (does not *have to* be deep) and not following proper *decompression* steps causing an *air embolism. Air embolism* can occur as air bubbles enter the blood stream and lodge in joints or in the brain. May have signs and symptoms similar to a stroke, joint pain, cough, pink or bloody frothy sputum, cyanosis, skin blotching, vision problems. **Baro-trauma** *is air pressure injury to the lungs* from breath-holding on ascent. **Decompression sickness**: also called "The Bends" or "Nitrogen narcosis" (the patient may act drunk or under the influence of narcotics.) While diving, small nitrogen bubbles form in the blood from the pressures at depth and must expand *gradually* as the diver follows strict rules to slowly return to the surface. If proper recompression is not followed *decompression sickness* may result as the too large bubbles block blood flow and cause other problems such as joint pain or itching (Diver's itch.)

442. Decompression chamber: *these are not commonly available devices.* A patient with *decompression sickness* can be placed in the chamber and the pressure is increased, causing the bubbles in the blood stream to become smaller and not dangerous, then the chamber can be *slowly* returned to normal pressure allowing the body to properly handle the gradually increasing bubbles, as if the diver had followed the proper steps to return to the surface.

443. Breath-holding syncope: skin divers may *hyperventilate* before entering the water to increase oxygen levels and allow a longer dive, but the breathing drive may not be triggered due to low carbon dioxide levels from the hyperventilation, causing the diver to use up the oxygen and pass out before feeling the need to take a breath. *Treat the same as drowning.*

444. HACE (High Altitude Cerebral Edema) and **HAPE** (High Altitude Pulmonary Edema): *Acute mountain sickness*, is a situation encountered my climbers, usually above 8000 feet in altitude. *Caused by diminished oxygen pressure in the air causing low oxygen in the blood.* A too-rapid ascent and climbers not becoming slowly acclimatized to the altitude are the main causes. *Swelling of the brain* and *fluid in the lungs* are the two main emergencies, and the cure is rapidly getting the patient to a lower altitude. Signs/Symptom: *headache, fatigue, loss of appetite, dizziness, trouble sleeping, shortness of breath, cough or cough with pink sputum, and swelling of the face.*

445. Lighting: Swimmers, boaters, and golfers are among the most common victims of the some 300 reported lightning strikes on humans each year. Cardiac and respiratory arrest is the common result of lightning strike. A case of multiple people struck by lightning will require a *reverse triage*, placing those patients in *cardiac arrest in the most immediate category for care.* The prompt use of a defibrillator may save these patients.

446. Black widow spider: The female spider is black with a distinctive red/orange hourglass marking on its abdomen. *The bite usually causes severe abdominal cramping and spasms.* Most dangerous to the old, sick, or young; most patients will survive with treatment of their symptoms until recovered.

447. Brown Recluse spider: Short-haired brown body with a violin shaped marking on its back (sometimes called Violin spider). Mostly in southern and central U.S. Causes sometimes severe local tissue damage; necrosis (death) of tissue.

448. Hymenoptera is the family of *bees, wasps, yellow jackets, and ants.* Painful but almost never dangerous. Remove the stinger and venom sac if present; scrape away with firm card. *Use ice packs for pain relief.* Allergic reaction may occur, a serious *anaphylactic reaction* can cause flushed skin, hives (urticaria), low blood pressure, trouble breathing (wheezing), swelling of tongue or throat. *EpiPen is a common treatment.*

449. Snake bites: Rare in the U.S., about 15 deaths per year. Use caution, that snake, or another may still be at the scene! Rattlesnakes, cottonmouths, and copperheads are all **pit vipers**; with *flat looking triangular heads.* Their fangs inject venom that may be *hemotoxic*, causing bleeding in tissues, or *neurotoxic* effecting the central nervous system. Expect severe pain at the site of the bite, swelling and ***ecchymosis*** (blue discoloration of skin).

450. Scorpion stings: painful but not dangerous stings, except some rare scorpions in the Southwest deserts or Arizona and New Mexico, Texas, Nevada, and parts of California, which can cause circulatory collapse and cardiac arrest, along with excessive salivation and convulsions.

451. Tick bites: ticks can be so small it looks like a freckle. They bite and burrow their heads into the skin. The danger comes from organisms carried by ticks causing diseases such as *Rocky Mountain Spotted Fever* and *Lyme Disease.* A tick can be removed with tweezers by gently grasping close to the head and lifting up slightly and holding it up until it releases its hold. *Crush and kill it after removal but do not come in direct skin contact with it.*

452. Jellyfish, Coral, Sea anemones have stinging cells. *Jellyfish* may most commonly be encountered; if *tentacles* are still attached to the patient they should be scraped off with a stiff card. The patient may have an *anaphylactic reaction*, but most commonly will experience localized pain, swelling, and redness. Jellyfish stinging cells, along with spines from urchins or stingrays can be deactivated by soaking in hot water (110-115 degrees F) which should relieve pain. *The patient should be transported for further wound care.*

453. Obstetrics: The *ovary* releases an egg which travels down the *fallopian tube* to the *uterus* where it implants and develops into an *embryo*, then a *fetus* (from 10 weeks until delivery). During *labor* the *cervix* (the opening from the uterus) dilates and a *mucous plug* is discharged from the *vagina* as pink-tinged mucous called the "bloody show."

454. Perineum: *the area between the vagina and the anus.*

455. Placenta: is attached to the *uterine wall* and provides nourishment to the *fetus* through the *umbilical cord*. The *umbilical cord* has two arteries and one vein. The *amniotic sac* is a membrane that forms at the outside edges of the *placenta* and is filled with 500 to 1000cc's of *amniotic fluid* surrounding the *fetus* which cushions and protects the *fetus*. When labor begins the pressure of *contractions* ruptures the *amniotic sac*. Part of the EMT's evaluation is to ask if the patient's "water broke" which often indicates that birth is imminent.

456. Preeclampsia or **Pregnancy induced hypertension:** the pregnant patient may develop hypertension, a persistent headache, visual disturbances, and swelling of hands and feet. **Eclampsia** is the development of *seizures* related to hypertension from pregnancy.

457. Supine hypotensive syndrome: the weight of the pregnant belly can compress the *inferior vena cava* when the patient lies *supine* which reduces blood flow to the heart. *Pregnant patients in the third trimester should be transported on their left side to prevent hypotension.*

458. Ectopic pregnancy: also known as a "tubal pregnancy" occurs when the fertilized egg implants in the **fallopian tube** and not the uterus. The pregnancy cannot be completed if this occurs, and a rupture of the **fallopian tube** can cause life-threatening bleeding. *Any woman who has missed a menstrual cycle with sudden severe lower abdominal pain should be suspected as having an ectopic pregnancy and should be promptly transported to the hospital.*

459. Abruptio placenta *and* **placenta previa:** In *abruptio placenta* the placenta *separates from the uterus too soon*, causing mostly internal bleeding with signs of shock with pain and a rigid abdomen even between contractions. In *placenta previa* the placenta is close to the cervix, maybe even obstructing the opening. When labor begins the placenta will tear and will result in heavy bleeding and pain. *Both of these conditions are life-threatening.*

460. Abortion: either *spontaneous* or *induced*; a spontaneous sudden loss of a baby before 20 weeks without a known cause is also called a *miscarriage*. An *induced* abortion may be a hospital procedure or done by the patient or someone else. *The EMT should save any products of conception that have been expelled and transport them to the hospital for inspection by the doctor.*

461. CPR on a pregnant patient: If the woman dies the baby will most likely die. *Do CPR like any other patient with two exceptions*: in late pregnancy *chest compression should be done slightly higher on the sternum*, and one of the rescuers should continuously *manually displace the uterus toward the patient's left side* to allow better blood flow to the heart.

462. Three stages of labor: (First stage) *Dilation*, from the onset of contractions until full dilation of the cervix, **(Second stage)** *Expulsion*, from the full dilation of the cervix to delivery of the baby, **(Third stage)** *Placental*, from delivery of the baby until the placenta delivers.

463. Crowning: when the top (vertex) of the baby's head can be seen at the vagina.

464. Fundus: the upper part of the *uterus*, felt as a firm mass the size of a grapefruit *in the lower abdomen*. Is *massaged* if excessive bleeding (more than 500cc) is present after delivery.

465. Apgar score: Newborns are evaluated in five areas (*Appearance, Pulse, Grimace, Activity, Respirations*) and are given either 0, 1, or 2 points; *a perfect Apgar score is 10*. Apgar is checked at **1 minute after the birth** and again at **5 minutes after the birth**. *Appearance* is evaluated based on the presence of *cyanosis*. It is common for newborns to have blueish (cyanotic) hands and feet shortly after birth, but the hands, feet, and mucous membranes should become pink quickly; points are deducted if cyanosis is present. *Pulse* is measured by chest *auscultation* (listening) or *palpated* (feeling) at the brachial pulse. *Grimace* or *irritability* is a measure of the newborn's crying and withdrawing reflex when snapping the sole of the newborn's foot. *Activity* or *muscle tone* is measured by attempting to straighten the newborn's legs and checking for their attempt to resist it; they should not be limp. *Respirations* should be regular, rapid, and the newborn should have a strong cry. *An Apgar score of 7-8 at 1 minute and 8-10 at 5 minutes is expected.*

	2	1	0
Appearance:	entire newborn is pink	hands & feet blue	all blue or pale
Pulse:	greater than 100	less than 100	no pulse
Grimace:	pulls away from foot snap	weak cry with stimulus	no cry or reaction

Activity:	2	1	0
resists leg straightening		weak resistance	limp
Respirations:	2	1	0
rapid		slow	absent

466. Blow-by oxygen for newborns: if the infant is breathing adequately you don't need to *assist* with a BVM. If they continue to show signs of *cyanosis*, but are breathing adequately, use *blow-by* oxygen by holding an oxygen mask set at **5 L/min.** close to their face. *(Avoid blowing oxygen into the eyes which can dry them and cause damage.)*

467. Assisting newborn breathing with a BVM: the *bag-valve-mask* device, which may be called a **BMD**, *Bag-mask-device*, should be used to breath for the infant when their breathing and/or *tidal volume* is not adequate. *Assist by giving 40 to 60 breaths/min.*

468. Vertex delivery: The *vertex* is the top of the head; it is most common for babies to be born head-first, which is called a ***vertex presentation***. A ***breech presentation*** is most commonly a buttocks first presentation or less commonly a feet-first presentation.

469. Breech birth: after the body delivers the head may be slow to deliver. With the body out the baby may attempt to breathe, and we should make a "V" near its face by inserting two fingers into the vagina to avoid obstruction of the mouth and nose and allow the baby to breathe. This and *prolapsed cord* are the only two times we should insert fingers into the vagina.

470. Prolapsed cord: *is when the umbilical cord comes out of the vagina before the baby.* This can cause compression of the cord and restrict blood supply to the baby. If birth is not imminent, place the mother supine and elevate her hips 12 inches to reduce the weight of the infant pressing on the cord; then place several fingers into the vagina and move the infant's head away from the cord and continue this enroute to the hospital. *Wrap a towel moistened with saline around the exposed cord.*

471. Presenting part: if a hand, foot, arm, or leg is coming out of the vagina before the baby we must transport quickly to the hospital. Elevate the hips to take pressure off the birth canal. Do not attempt to push a part back into the mother. *The baby cannot be delivered vaginally if there is a presenting part!*

472. Spina Bifida: a defect where a portion of the spinal cord or meninges protrudes outside of the vertebrae or outside of the body on the lumbar area of the back. Cover the exposed spinal cord with a moist sterile dressing and then an *occlusive* dressing; this area is very susceptible to infection.

473. Fetal demise: a baby that has died before birth may have a foul odor when delivered or may show other signs of *decomposition* such as skin blisters or skin sloughing off and dark discoloration. The head is often very soft and perhaps deformed. Such "obviously dead" infants should NOT undergo resuscitation effort. *Of course, normal appearing newborns in cardiac arrest should be vigorously resuscitated.*

474. Delivery without an OB Kit: if an OB Kit is not available, such as assisting with a birth when off-duty, use clean sheets or clean cloths to dry the baby and to wrap the baby to keep it warm. You DO NOT need to cut the umbilical cord under these conditions; simply wrap the placenta in a cloth and place in a plastic bag if available and keep it at the level of the baby during transport.

475. Postpartum hemorrhage: *bleeding of **more than 500cc** after deliver of the placenta* is considered life-threatening. We can help the uterus to contract with **fundal massage** and by **allowing the baby to breast feed**; as the uterus contracts the bleeding should slow then stop. *Continue fundal massage in route with immediate transport if bleeding is not controlled.*

476. Pulmonary embolism after childbirth: there is an increased risk of a blood clot blocking the pulmonary circulation after childbirth. If the patient suddenly complains of difficulty breathing, give oxygen, treat for shock as needed, and transport immediately. *Pulmonary embolism related to childbirth may occur days or weeks after the birth!*

477. Imminent birth: the EMT must assess if childbirth is *imminent*, may occur within minutes, or if the woman is simply in labor and transport rather than delivery at the scene is indicated. Signs of imminent birth are strong *contractions lasting approximately 45 seconds occurring about every 2 minutes, the urge to push and/or the urge to have a bowel movement, and of course* **crowning** *when the baby is visible at the vagina.*

478. Cord around the neck: if the umbilical cord is around the baby's neck it may be loose enough to lift over the head and out of the way; if it is tight and cannot be removed from around the neck it must be clamped in two places about 2 inches apart and cut.

479. Amniotic sac around the baby's head: if a portion of the amniotic sac, which may be filled with water, is around the baby's head it must be removed. Pinch the amniotic sac and tear it to remove from the baby's head.

480. Gravida: *the number of times the patient has been pregnant in her entire life.*

481. Para: the number of *live births* the patient has ever had.

482. Pediatrics: *specialized medical care for children.* **Infants** are *up until 3 years old*, then they are then called **Toddlers**. **Preschool-age** is *from 3-6*, **school-age** *from 6-12*, **adolescents** *from 12-18*.

483. Fontanelles: the *soft spots* at the front and back of an infant's head do not grow together until about 18 months old for the front area and until about 6 months for the posterior. A *sunken fontanelle* can be a sign of dehydration.

484. Pediatric Assessment Triangle (PAT): *is a quick assessment tool to help evaluate in the first 30 seconds if a child is sick or not sick.* **Appearance**, do they have good muscle tone and mental status. **Work of breathing**, are they using accessory muscles to help them breath in the chest, *supraclavicular contractions* under the clavicles or retractions of the muscles between the ribs called *intercostal retractions* or under the sternum called *substernal retractions*, or tensing of muscles of the neck, or sucking in of the abdomen, are they making "grunting" noises when breathing, do they have "nasal flaring" or "head bobbing" where they lift their head to breath and the head goes forward to exhale. **Circulation to the skin**, pallor (paleness), mottling, or cyanosis (blueish skin) is a bad sign in an infant.

485. Tripod position: sitting leaning forward with arms out to the side supporting is often a sign of respiratory distress in children and adults.

486. Sniffing position: opening the airway of the pediatric patient is best accomplished using the *sniffing position*, just slightly tilted back from the neutral position. *Hyperextending* the head is generally OK with older children and adults but with younger children such aggressive extension of the neck can block the airway. *A folded towel about 1 inch thick placed under the shoulders and upper back will achieve a sniffing position.*

487. Infants and children and hypothermia: keep pediatric patients warm when sick or injured, they are prone to become hypothermic more easily than adults.

488. Asthma: when assisting breathing in a pediatric asthma patient, *use slow gentle breaths with the BVM.* Asthma will make the exhalation of air difficult, and we must allow time for exhalation. *Avoid rapid or forceful use of the BVM.*

489. Croup: an infection of the airway below the vocal cords caused by a virus. Most common in children from 6 months to 3 years old. *Stridor* (high-pitched crowing sound) with a seal-like deep cough. Use humidified oxygen if available. *Bronchodilators are NOT advised* and could make these children worse!

490. Epiglottitis: *infection of the epiglottis just above the vocal cords;* usually from a bacteria. Mostly seen in infants and young children. The swelling of the epiglottitis can obstruct the airway. Child often sits forward (tripod position), has a fever, and drools to avoid painful swallowing. *Do not make these children cry, limit exam and transport quickly with blow-by oxygen.*

491. Broselow tape, *also called* **"Length-based resuscitation tape"** is a pediatric measurement device to determine a child's approximate weight to estimate the correct dose of medications and the proper size of equipment such as airway adjuncts.

492. Oxygen delivery: *Room air is about 21% oxygen.* **Blow-by oxygen** is used when putting a mask or cannula on an infant or child may be impossible; the mask with 6 L/min. of O2 is held near the child's mouth (avoid blowing oxygen into the eyes.) This method delivers *more than 21% oxygen*. The **nasal cannula** set between 1-6 L/min. provides *24-44% oxygen*. A **non-rebreather face mask** set at 10-15 L/min. will deliver about *95% oxygen*. The **BVM** at 15 L/min. provides *about 100% oxygen* with assisted ventilations.

493. Child abuse: we should be on the look-out for suspicious complaints and injuries involving children that may indicate possible child abuse. *Unusual bruises, burns, fractures, confusion, dirty clothing or dirty or dangerous living conditions. Report immediately to proper authorities.*

494. Sudden Infant Death Syndrome (SIDS): an unexplained death of an infant or child. Infants should be placed on their back to sleep on a firm mattress with no bumpers, blankets, or toys. The suspicion is that an object close to the baby's face allows the build-up of carbon dioxide which can cause sudden respiratory arrest leading to cardiac arrest.

495. Apparent Life-Threatening Event (ALTE): infants who have been found with cyanosis and apnea (not breathing) or who have become cyanotic and become limp but who soon resume breathing, and may even have little or no distress upon the arrival of EMS, have experienced an **ALTE**. *Such patients should be transported to the hospital for further evaluation!*

496. Geriatrics: *the assessment and treatment of patients over 65 years old.* Do not assume older patients are hard of hearing. Be patient with patients who need more time to answer your questions or collect their thoughts.

497. Arteriosclerosis: *hardening of the arteries,* may be caused by various disease conditions along with aging.

498. Atherosclerosis: *fat and cholesterols plaques building up in arteries.* Can weaken arteries leading to ***aneurysm***, a bulging of a weakened artery that may then rupture.

499. Postural hypotension (Orthostatic hypotension): *a condition where a change in position can drop the blood pressure;* such as having a dizzy patient suddenly stand up to get on your gurney.

500. DVT (Deep Vein Thrombosis): blood clots in veins that can lead to pulmonary embolism.

501. Heart failure: *Right-sided heart failure,* ***fluid backs up into the body;*** jugular vein distention, ***ascites*** (fluid in the abdomen). Sometimes from an enlarged liver. *Right-sided heart failure* can be caused by *left-sided heart failure.* With *left-sided heart failure* ***fluid backs up into the lungs,*** causing *pulmonary edema,* shortness of breath and *rales* (crackles) in the lungs. These patients have sudden respiratory distress when reclining or sleeping (**paroxysmal nocturnal dyspnea**) and begin coughing and have a tachycardia. **Orthopnea** is *the term for difficulty breathing when lying down.* Asking "Do you sleep sitting up" can help to determine a history of *orthopnea.*

502. Stroke: CVA or *Cerebral Vascular Accident* is a *stroke.* A stroke is caused by either a blocked artery in the brain or a ruptured artery in the brain (*Ischemic* or *Hemorrhagic* stroke). Slurred speech, one-sided weakness or paralysis, visual disturbance, headache, dizziness, incontinence, or seizure are all possible signs or symptoms. Often related to high blood pressure. *Transport time is critical as well as transport to a Stroke Center if possible.*

503. Cataracts: *a clouding of the lens of the eye or cornea.*

504. Dementia: a slow onset of brain dysfunction that may be caused by Alzheimer's disease, Parkinson's disease, CVA, or genetic predisposition. Patients often become confused, delusional or aggressive, lose the ability to think properly (cognitive functions), become less mobile and lose many of their social skills.

505. Syncope (fainting): always considered a possible life-threat in geriatric patients, and always taken very seriously in ALL patients.

506. Neuropathy: diabetics and other patients may relate a history of *neuropathy*, which is a nerve disorder of the peripheral nerves. *Loss of balance, pain, muscle weakness, cramps, tingling, itching, sensitivity to touch, heat, or cold, and changes in blood pressure, heart rate, bladder function, and more, can all be symptoms.*

507. Melena: *black, tarry stools from bleeding that has traveled through the digestive system* and is expelled. *Partially digested blood* may be vomited out as **"coffee-ground emesis"** and appear as brown or black flaky material.

508. Bowel obstruction: more common in older patients due to the slowing of *peristalsis* (the muscular movement of the intestines to move food along) and changes in diet and consumption of liquids. *Syncope* while straining on the toilet is a common occurrence in older populations, due to constipation or bowel obstruction. Bearing down during a bowel movement can raise the blood pressure which can trigger the *vagus* nerve to slow the heart rate (a *vasovagal response*), causing fainting. Once the patient is supine, they will probably regain consciousness.

509. Kyphosis (forward curving of the spine, also called *hunchback* or *humpback*) common in elderly patients.

510. Osteoporosis: *a decrease in bone mass* causing a weakening of the bone and a susceptibility to fractures.

511. Decubitus ulcers (bed sores): a breakdown of the skin from constant pressure, exposure to urine, and lack of movement. Common in bed-ridden patients. Painful, hard to heal, prone to infection. *Can be a sign of elder abuse form lack of proper care.*

512. Polypharmacy: *a term for multiple medications used by one patient.* Can be dangerous in patients who see several different doctors and the doctors are not all familiar with the various treatments of the other physicians; causing overdosing or negative interactions between various medications. *Bring ALL the patient's medications to the hospital for review by the physician.*

513. Behavioral emergencies: various causes, phycological and physical can lead to depression, suicide or suicidal thoughts. *The EMT 'should' ask if the patient wants to kill themselves and or if they have a plan on how to do it.* This ensures that those contemplating suicide **will** be transported and receive intervention. If the potentially suicidal patient refuses transport, we will involve the police to place the patient on a '5150 hold' and force transport since they are a possible danger to themselves and others.

514. The GEMS Diamond: an assessment tool for geriatric patients that could be helpful in remembering the special considerations when dealing with the elderly. **G- Geriatric**, to remind you that dealing with the elderly involves some special concerns. **E- Environmental assessment**, to make note of living conditions and safety concerns. **M- Medical assessment**, including numerous medications, OTC (over the counter) meds, and even herbal medications or supplements. **S- Social assessment**, social activities, dressing, eating. *Your assessment of these GEMS topics could lead to a notification to the hospital regarding your special concerns and could lead to a referral for the patient to address these issues.*

515. Don't remove dentures: unless they create an airway problem; generally, it will be easier to ventilate a patient with their dentures in place.

516. Bleeding issues in the elderly: several heart and other conditions are treated using blood thinners such as warfarin/coumadin, or heparin, which can cause serious bleeding issues following trauma.

517. MRSA (Methicillin-resistant Staphylococcus aureus): common in nursing facilities and hospitals, and easily spread, these dangerous infections are difficult to treat since they are resistant to most known antibiotics. *EMS personnel must practice the use of PPEs, good handwashing, proper disposal of contaminated items, and proper cleaning and disinfection of all EMS equipment and the ambulance.*

518. Advanced directives: such as "living wills" are legal documents to address treatment issues in the event the patient cannot speak or make such decisions. **DNR**, *Do Not Resuscitate*, is a common issue EMT personnel must determine. If the patient has a valid DNR order, we will NOT resuscitate them from respiratory or cardiac arrest. Such patients usually have a **DNR** order because of a *terminal illness* and they have decided not to undergo resuscitative measures. Other documents might detail what specific treatments the patient desires and others they do not, such as a **POLST** (*Physicians Order for Life-Saving Treatment*) might detail. *If we are unsure if a DNR order is valid, we should immediately begin to resuscitate.*

519. Elder abuse, like child abuse, has specific reporting requirements that may vary from place to place. *Our goal is to ensure the safety of our patients if we suspect abuse or neglect is occurring.* Follow local protocols and do NOT ignore issues related to the safety and well-being of our patients. *Report such concerns immediately to your supervisor or other proper authorities.*

520. Developmental disability: autism, Down syndrome, brain injury and other issues may affect a person's ability to interact with others or to effectively participate in the EMT's questioning and evaluation process. *We should be patient with patients who show signs of some disability.* Although we **do** want to interact with and discuss what we are doing with the patient, we may need to gather much of our assessment information from a family member or caretaker.

521. Service animals can and should accompany the patient into the ambulance and hospital.

522. Cerebral palsy: a brain injury in utero (in the uterus) or during birthing, or an infection such as meningitis in young childhood, causing spastic movements of extremities, poor posture, speech trouble, possible hearing problems, and may affect intellect.

523. Morbid obesity: *patients of extreme and health-adverse weight.* Ask the patient how best to move them. Avoid putting excessive strain on any one joint. Work together with your team to move the patient and have appropriate additional manpower. Avoid placing patient *supine*, which may make it difficult for them to breathe. Avoid pinching patient on moving parts of gurney. Notify the receiving hospital of the patient to allow them to prepare equipment and additional manpower.

524. Tracheostomy: *a surgical opening in the neck creating a stoma,* a hole providing direct access to the *trachea*. A *stoma* may have a plastic *tracheostomy tube* inserted. Tubes may develop *mucus obstructions* that must be suctioned clear; water may be added to loosen secretions. To apply oxygen, place an oxygen mask over the opening in the neck.

525. Implanted defibrillator/pacemaker: usually a small lump in the upper chest. When placing defibrillator patches do not put the patch directly over the implanted device, move at least an inch away from it. *Do CPR and use your AED/defibrillator as you normally would with any other patient.*

526. LVAD (Left Ventricular Assist Devices): a device used to pump blood for a defective heart; these patients may be waiting for a heart transplant. If present, family members should know specific information about dealing with the LVAD. *Your local authority may have special protocols for dealing with these devices.*

527. Central venous catheters: (central line) usually in the upper chest subclavian area, these catheters are inserted into the vena cava to provide access to the central circulation for medications or dialysis. If there is bleeding, apply pressure and transport.

528. Gastrostomy tubes: *G-tube,* or *"feeding tube"* usually inserted into the nose and to the stomach for giving nutrition to patients who cannot eat or drink. *Transport the patient sitting or lying on their right side with their head elevated 30 degrees to prevent aspiration.*

529. Shunt: a drain to remove excess *cerebral spinal fluid* (CSF) from the brain to prevent pressure building up. A blocked shut can cause a bulging Fontenelle and a high-pitched cry in an infant, headache, fever, nausea, vomiting, blurred vision, seizure, bradycardia, and dysthymias. *Immediate transport is required.*

530. Colostomy or **ileostomy:** a surgical opening from the small or large intestine to the surface of the body for the elimination of waste. The opening is called a *stoma.* Feces are expelled into a bag which is emptied or changed frequently.

531. Types of ambulances: Type 1, a truck with an ambulance compartment attached. ***Type 2****, a standard van type ambulance.* **Type 3**, a box-type attachment on a standard van chassis.

532. Siren risk vs. benefit: unless your service mandates certain levels of response, the EMT must evaluate the benefit of using their siren vs. the risk that siren use might pose to the patient. Responding to an emergency call it is common to always drive Code 3 (lights and siren). *When transporting it is common for the* <u>*EMT to decide whether or not to transport Code 3*</u>. Transport times may be so short that using a siren to "save time" makes no sense.

The use of the siren is likely to raise the anxiety of your patient, including their pulse, breathing rate, and blood pressure. The risk of being involved in a vehicle collision increases when driving Code 3. *Use good judgment as to when to drive Code 3 and when you should just drive.* You must be driving Code 3, with proper lights on and the siren on if you intend to travel faster than the speed limit or violate any other regular "rules of the road." *ALWAYS drive your ambulance with "due regard" for the safety of you, your patient, and all others on the roadway.*

533. Air ambulances and **medivac:** *the use of helicopters in EMS transport will follow local protocols.* Several important considerations go along with the use of a helicopter; deciding on a safe landing zone, the presence of obstructions such as buildings, trees, power lines. The presence of loose debris or equipment in the landing area that will be thrown by rotor wash. As a rule, you NEVER approach a helicopter until instructed to do so by the helicopter crew! NEVER approach from the rear of the helicopter where the tail rotor may be at head level and invisible while spinning! Use caution if the ground is not level, a slight mound or elevation may place your head at the level of main rotor blade!

534. Vehicle extrication: it is most often the fire department with their specialized equipment that will handle most difficult extrications from vehicles. As an EMT you can use common sense and available tools to affect an extrication when safely possible, such as breaking a window to gain access (taking care where glass will be thrown). *Local rules and protocols should discuss extrication issues in general and will dictate whether you can force entry into a home or whether that should be left to police or fire.*

535. Air bags: *delayed deployment of airbags may occur some time after a vehicle accident and have caused deaths!* The fire department will often disconnect the battery of vehicles to ensure sparks don't occur and that the power to fire an airbag is disconnected. *Use caution when working in the interior of a vehicle after a crash.*

536. Extreme hazards: depending on the incident, there may be a *safe zone* and a *danger* **zone** or *hot zone*. We generally *keep our ambulance in the safe zone* and should be sure it is safe to do so before entering the hot zone.

537. Electric cars: several specialized batteries are used for electric vehicles. In a collision the batteries may leak or catch fire releasing dangerous fumes. *Use caution not to breathe any fumes.*

538. Incident commander: in large or specialized incidents there will be a designated *incident commander*. Arriving units should be instructed to report to the *incident commander* at a designated location (command post) for instructions, to avoid units "freelancing" and adding to an already chaotic situation. You should become familiar with the *Multi-Casualty-Incident system* your company or agency uses to handle and **MCI**.

539. Downed power lines: *always treat a fallen power line as if it is energized.* The power may be out but recycle back on at any time! A live wire in contact with a vehicle, as an example, may not harm people sitting in the car (they are insulated from the ground by the car tires). If those people step out of the vehicle and 'ground' themselves, they may be instantly electrocuted. Do not approach any scene with downed lines until the fire department or electrical utility has made it safe.

540. Arriving first at the scene of a fire: *do not rush into a smoky building on fire.* One breath of heavy smoke is likely to render you unconscious. We generally will not have the appropriate safety equipment to enter a dangerous environment. *Wait for the appropriately equipped rescuers to arrive!*

541. Mutual aid: is the concept that surrounding agencies will assist their neighboring jurisdictions in the event of an incident that overwhelms the local system.

542. Triage: *the sorting out of patients* to determine which patients are most serious and should be treated first.

543. Triage categories: the four common triage categories are; **Immediate** (red), **Delayed** (yellow), **Minor** (green), **Morgue** or *Expectant* (black).

Note: I don't believe that you should necessarily memorize the START system below. Your service may use some other method to triage. But read this, and be familiar with it for possible test questions on the National Registry Test.

544. The START triage system: *Step one* determines the *"walking wounded"* who can follow commands and are ambulatory (can walk). Those people are moved out of the immediate area to a nearby landmark to wait. The remaining patients are quickly triaged and tagged as follows: Not breathing, open their airway with a *head-tilt.* If they do not breathe, they are tagged *Morgue* (black). If they breathe, tag them *Immediate* (red), place them on their side in *recovery position* and move on to the next patient. For breathing patients; faster than 30 breaths/min. or slower than 10 breaths/min. tag *Immediate* (red). If the patient is breathing 10-29 breaths/min. move to next assessment step. The next step checks for proper circulation by checking *bilateral radial pulses.* Absent radial pulse, tag *Immediate* (red). If radial pulse is present, go to next step. Final assessment step assesses *neurological status.* Can they follow simple command such as "Show me three fingers." Those who cannot follow simple command are tagged *Immediate* (red), patients who can follow command are tagged *Delayed* (yellow).

545. Casualty collection area: in a large disaster or multiple casualty incident where triage at the scene is not possible, or in the event of a widespread area of devastation, the injured may be asked to go to, or may be transported to a *casualty collection area* where they will then be triaged.

546. HazMat: special *hazardous materials response units* are equipped and trained to handle dangerous materials. Call for HazMat whenever you believe a hazardous chemical or substance is involved or has the potential to be released.

547. DOT (Dept. of Transportation) *placards.* The diamond-shaped warning and identification *placards* are common on trucks and other vehicles or containers with certain amounts of hazardous materials. *Your company or agency may have a book for you to use as a reference to understand the markings on HazMat placards.*

548. MSDS (Material Safety Data Sheets): industrial buildings should have MSDS available to you showing details about the chemical or substance your patient may have been exposed to. If available, have someone get you that MSDS. *We should stay OUT of the immediate area of the hazard and wait for properly equipped personnel to work inside the danger zone.*

549. Warm zone, area where people move in and out of the **hot zone** (contaminated area), entry should be limited. **Decontamination area**, with limited numbers of specially equipped personnel to decontaminate patients. **Cold zone**, the *safe area* where no special clothing is needed. *The EMT should work in the cold zone to treat or transport patients.*

550. Terrorism: *International* (mostly outside of the U.S.) or *domestic* (inside the U.S.): bombings, the use of WMD's or *Weapons of Mass Destruction*, or other methods of causing the most damage or carnage to instill fear in the service of some usually radical agenda. Use the mnemonic **B-NICE** for the kinds of weapons of mass destruction; **B**iologic, **N**uclear, **I**ncendiary, **C**hemical, and **E**xplosive. Chemical agents are: *Vesicants* (blister agents), *Respiratory agents* (choking agents), *Nerve agents*, and *Metabolic agents* (cyanides).

551. Scene safety: stay upwind and uphill from a contaminated area. *Secondary devices* are sometimes planted to injure responders. *Do not enter areas of danger if possible.*

552. Cross-contamination: spreading contaminants through contact with someone or something that has not been decontaminated.

Note: I would not necessarily memorize all the types of hazardous agents and their actions on the body. But the National Registry could ask specific questions on some of these subjects.

553. Vesicants (blister agents): mustard gas, lewisite, phosgene oxime. **Pulmonary agents** (choking agents) chlorine, phosgene. **Nerve agents** (organophosphates) G agents, Sarin, Soman, Tabun, V agent. *Nerve agents may be treated with multiple doses of atropine and pralidoxime chloride.* **Metabolic agents**, cyanide. **Biologic agents** may be viruses or other diseases or bacteria such as *anthrax*.

554. Advanced airways: EMTs *could* use advanced airways and some other Paramedic procedures if the local *Medial Director* authorized it. Unless trained, the EMT will not place advanced airways in patients but will *ventilate patients* with advanced airways put in place by Paramedics. Several types of advanced airways will have a small tube with a small balloon on it attached to the device and visible outside of the patient's mouth. This "pilot balloon" should be inflated, with shows that the balloon at the distal end of the airway is also inflated. *The EMT must notify the Paramedic crew if the pilot balloon is deflated.* Advanced airways are inserted to a precise depth and should be secured by a strap or tape to keep it in proper position; the EMT using the airway to ventilate with the BVM should take care not to push the airway in deeper or pull it out further. *Notify the Paramedic if this occurs.*

555. The EMT will set up IV bags and tubing for the Paramedics as part of the EMS team. *Aseptic technique* refers to making sure that pathogens (germs) are not introduced onto any of the equipment during the process of opening and assembling sterile IV solutions or IV tubing. *If at any time contamination occurs, no matter how slight, notify the Paramedic and get replacement items and start again.*

556. "Spiking the bag" is a slang term for inserting the pointed *spike* of the IV tubing into the IV solution bag port.

The Heart

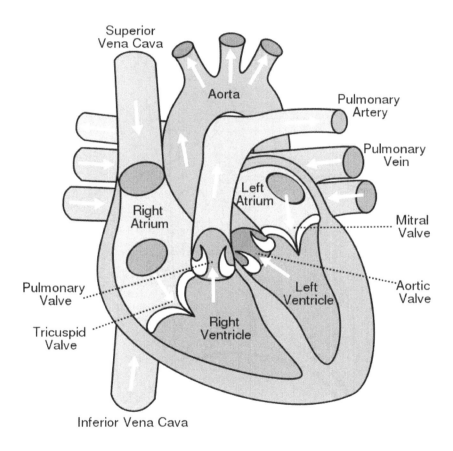

The Respiratory System

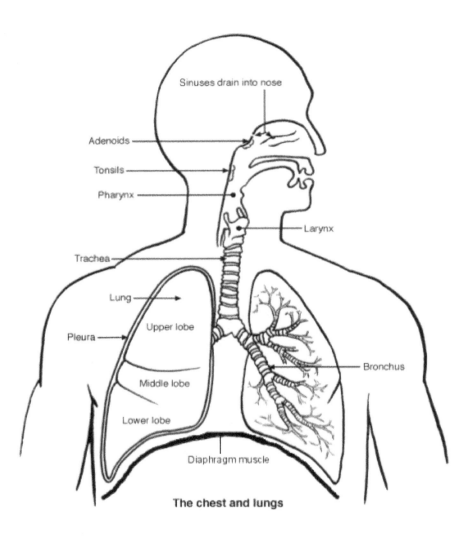

Sinuses drain into nose

Adenoids

Tonsils

Pharynx

Larynx

Trachea

Lung

Upper lobe

Pleura

Middle lobe

Lower lobe

Bronchus

Diaphragm muscle

The chest and lungs

Lobes of the brain

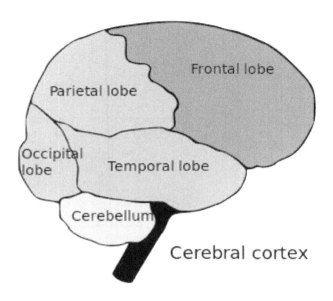

The skin

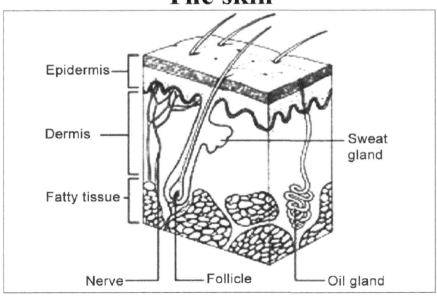

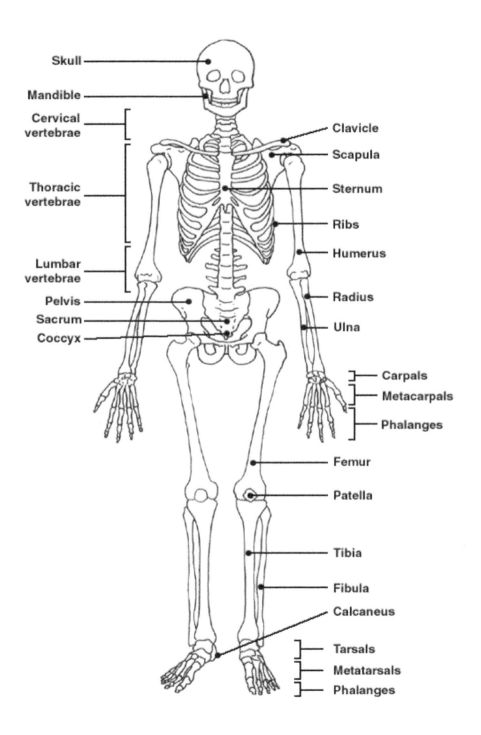

Skull

Mandible

Cervical
vertebrae

Thoracic
vertebrae

Lumbar
vertebrae

Pelvis

Sacrum

Coccyx

Clavicle

Scapula

Sternum

Ribs

Humerus

Radius

Ulna

Carpals

Metacarpals

Phalanges

Femur

Patella

Tibia

Fibula

Calcaneus

Tarsals

Metatarsals

Phalanges

Ventricular Fibrillation

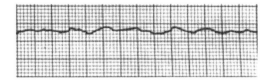

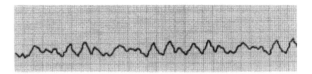

Fine or Coarse

Ventricular Tachycardia, V-Tach

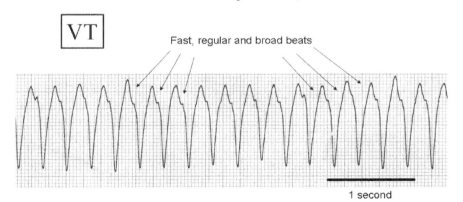

VT

Fast, regular and broad beats

1 second

Ventricular fibrillation, defibrillator shock, followed by asystole

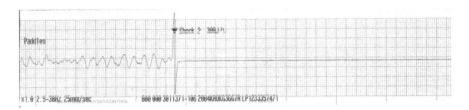

Normal Sinus Rhythm

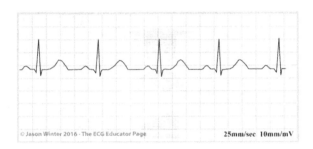

Electrical conduction in the heart

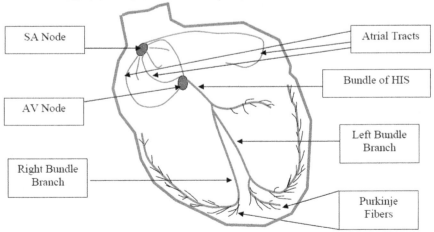

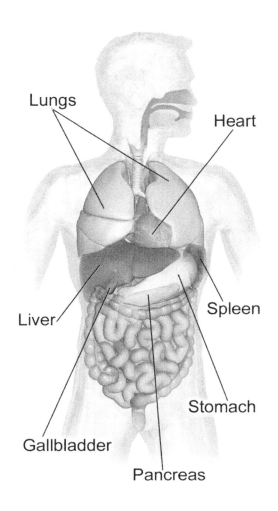

Lungs

Heart

Liver

Spleen

Gallbladder

Stomach

Pancreas

Conditions Associated with
Abdominal Pain

Right	Center	Left
Gallstones	Heartburn/indigestion	Functional dyspepsia
Cholecystitis	Hiatal hernia	Gastritis
Stomach ulcer	Epigastric hernia	Stomach ulcer
Duodenal ulcer	Stomach ulcer	Pancreatitis
Hepatitis	Duodenal ulcer	
	Hepatitis	
Kidney stones	Umbilical hernia	Kidney stones
Kidney infection	Early appendicitis	Kidney infection
Inflammatory bowel disease	Stomach ulcer	Inflammatory bowel disease
Constipation	Inflammatory bowel disease	Constipation
	Pancreatitis	
Appendicitis	Bladder infection	Constipation
Inflammatory bowel disease	Prostatitis	Irritable bowel syndrome
Constipation	Diverticulitis	Inflammatory bowel disease
Pelvic pain (Gyne)	Inflammatory bowel disease	Pelvic pain (Gyne)
	Inguinal hernia (groin pain)	Inguinal hernia (groin pain)
	Pelvic pain (Gyne)	

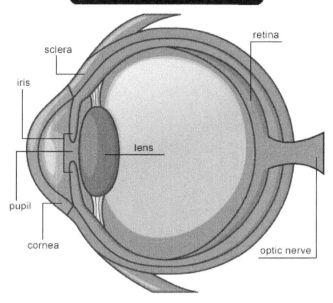

DIAGRAM OF THE EYE

The ear

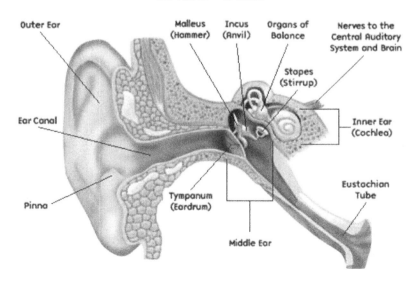

LARYNX AND VOCAL CORDS

Nasopharynx

Oropharynx

Tongue

Epiglottis

Vocal cords

Larynx

Trachea

Esophagus

Laryngopharynx

View from above

Tongue

Epiglottis

Vocal cord

Trachea

Esophagus

Vocal cords open while breathing and close while speaking.

Bones of the Skull - Side View

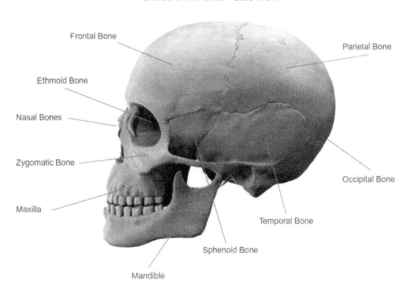

Frontal Bone

Parietal Bone

Ethmoid Bone

Nasal Bones

Zygomatic Bone

Occipital Bone

Maxilla

Temporal Bone

Sphenoid Bone

Mandible

The Spinal Column

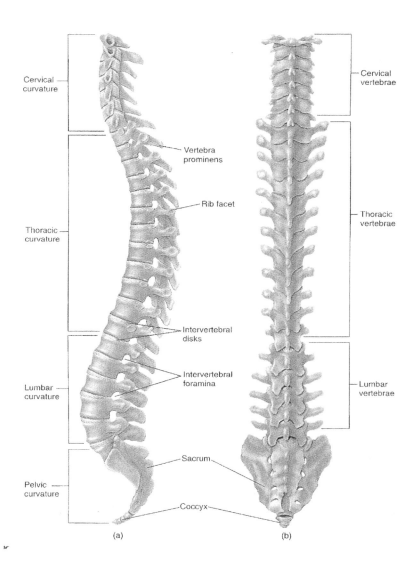

Cervical curvature

Vertebra prominens

Rib facet

Thoracic curvature

Intervertebral disks

Intervertebral foramina

Lumbar curvature

Sacrum

Pelvic curvature

Coccyx

(a)

Cervical vertebrae

Thoracic vertebrae

Lumbar vertebrae

(b)

This book is designed to **STUDY**.
Learning this material will require you to
re-read this book several, perhaps MANY
times. You are *memorizing* a large amount of
information; that's how you'll know the
right answers to test questions! Work hard,
review and study this book repeatedly
throughout your EMT course!

You're on your way to becoming a certified EMT!

QUESTIONS: *(Taken from pages 17-36)*

1. What is the medical term for the heart muscle?

2. Name the four pumping chambers of the heart.

3. Which chamber of the heart is the main pumping chamber?

4. Which vessels are the high-pressure vessels, carrying *oxygenated* blood?

5. Which vessels are low-pressure vessels and carry *deoxygenated* blood?

6. When does an *artery* carry *deoxygenated* blood and a *vein* carry *oxygenated* blood?

7. Deoxygenated blood *gets to* the right atrium from the lower parts of the body through what vessels?

8. Blood gets to the right atrium from the upper parts of the body through which vessels?

9. *Inferior* means what?

10. *Superior* means what?

11. What is the name of the largest veins in the body?

12. The heart is divided into the right and left heart by what?

13. Where does the *right heart* pump blood to?

14. Blood travels through what vessel to get to the lungs?

15. Any vessel carrying blood *away* from the heart is called what?

16. Blood going *back to* the heart travels in what sort of vessel?

17. After leaving the *left atrium* blood passes through what valve?

18. What is the main pumping chamber of the heart?

19. What is the largest artery in the body?

20. The largest artery in the body branches out into smaller vessels called what?

21. The smallest vessels carrying oxygenated blood are called what?

22. Which vessels have walls so thin that gasses and nutrients can pass through and get into the surrounding tissues?

23. What term describes a vessels ability to allow gasses and nutrients to pass through them?

24. What is the name of the smallest vessels that take blood back toward the heart?

25. The largest veins in the body are called what?

26. What is the medical term for a "Heart Attack?"

27. What term means *death of tissue*?

28. Name five signs or symptoms of a heart attack.

29. What does the term *diaphoresis* mean?

30. What is the preferred method of delivering oxygen to a patient with a possible heart attack?

31. What is a "sign?"

32. What is a "symptom?"

33. List four signs or symptoms of a possible heart attack that are more common in women than in men.

34. Specifically, what is *Coronary Artery Disease?*

35. What does *Ventricular Fibrillation* mean?

36. What is the difference between **Clinical death** *and* **Biological death**?

37. What is another term for Cardiac Arrest?

38. What does the term AED stand for?

39. What does an AED do?

40. What does the term *asystole* mean?

41. What signs or symptoms would you expect in a patient with *Angina*?

42. What common cardiac medication *dilates* all arteries?

43. Name two side affects you might expect with the above medication.

44. Before taking nitroglycerin, the patient should lay down, to avoid the effect of this **vasodilation**. *(Vaso refers to vessels.)*

45. Name three medications that an EMT may assist a patient with.

46. How many lobes does the **right lung** have?

47. How many lobes does the **left lung** have?

48. What is the waste gas that is expelled from the lungs?

49. Name the main airway connected to the nose and mouth.

50. Name the branches of the airways going to each lung.

51. What does the term *oral pharynx* mean?

52. Name the flap of tissue which is right next to the *vocal cords*.

53. Immediately past the vocal cords is the entrance into what?

54. Name one of the advanced airways used by Paramedics.

55. What is the term for a 'sudden' medical problem?

56. What is the term for a 'long term' medical problem?

57. What does the medical term SOB stand for?

58. What might cause a *physical obstruction* of the airway?

59. What might cause an *anatomical obstruction* of the airway?

60. What does "positive pressure" breathing mean?

61. What is considered a normal breathing rate?

62. What does *tidal volume* mean?

63. What is the term for a bluish skin color?

64. Describe how you would do a head-tilt chin-lift.

65. The tongue is attached to the what part of the jaw?

66. What is the medical term for an open airway?

67. When would you use high-flow oxygen?

68. When would you use low-flow oxygen?

69. Which airways can constrict usually causing *wheezing*?

70. What does an *albuterol* inhaler do?

71. What is the medical term for a *severe allergic reaction*?

72. Name three possible signs of a severe allergic reaction.

73. What common lung problem is caused from damage to the air sacs of the lungs?

74. What is the medial term for the 'air sacs' in the lungs?

75. What is a medical term for *difficulty breathing?*

76. What does COPD mean?

77. What is the term to describe how someone might speak with severe shortness of breath?

78. What is the name of the oxygen delivery device that goes into a person's nostrils, and what is the recommended flow rate?

79. What device or devices can be used to deliver *High-flow oxygen* and what is the recommended flow rate?

80. What is one potential negative result of delivering high flow oxygen to a patient with emphysema?

81. What device can measure a patient's *blood levels of oxygen?*

82. What respiratory problem can be caused by enlarged mucus glands?

83. What does the term **sputum** mean?

84. In general, what position should we place patients in with difficulty breathing?

85. What device uses high-flow oxygen to assistance a patient's breathing using positive pressure?

86. What breathing problem can be caused by *left-sided* **heart** failure?

87. What does the term "rales" mean and what is another name for rales?

88. What does the term *auscultation* mean?

89. List three signs or symptoms you might expect with CHF.

90. What does the term *orthopnea* mean?

91. If a patient you have sitting up for some reason and they suddenly become unresponsive, what should you do?

92. What is a *pneumothorax*?

93. What is a *tension pneumothorax*?

94. What does *tracheal deviation* mean?

95. What is a term for a hole into the chest cavity with air and/or blood moving in and out of the wound with breaths?

96. What is a treatment for the above condition?

97. Name two types of strokes?

98. What signs or symptoms should you expect from a stroke?

99. What is the best position to place a stroke patient in?

100. How many sections do we divide the abdomen into when assessing it, and what landmark do we use to divide it?

101. List four organs in the right upper quadrant of the abdomen.

102. List three organs in the left upper quadrant of the abdomen.

103. List four organs in the right lower quadrant of the abdomen.

104. List three organs in the left lower quadrant of the abdomen.

105. A term for abnormal pouches in the intestine, causing pain.

106. A term for inflammation of the *gallbladder*.

107. What abdominal condition can cause "**referred pain**?"

108. What condition often causes an inflammation/infection in the right lower quadrant?

109. A dangerous ballooning of the aorta, felt as a pulsating mass may be a condition called?

110. What does the ***endocrine system*** do?

111. ***Perfusion*** means?

112. Define "shock."

113. What is one rapid treatment for shock?

114. ***Supine*** means what?

115. ***Fowler's*** position means what?

116. A preferred position for a patient with ***Altered Level Of Consciousness***?

117. In what position should you place someone with trouble breathing?

118. In what position should you place someone with a possible stroke?

119. In what position should you place someone with nausea or vomiting?

120. In what position should you place someone with a possible head injury?

121. In what position should you place someone who is dizzy?

122. In what position should you place someone who is confused?

123. In what position should you place someone who is pale, cool, and sweaty?

124. In what position should you place someone who is unconscious?

125. In what position should you place someone with a slow or no pulse?

126. In what position should you place someone with a low blood pressure?

127. In what position should you place someone who you are about to give nitroglycerin?

128. If we sit someone up but then they get dizzy, or pass out, what do we do?

129. If we laid someone down, and then they have trouble breathing, what do we do?

130. What is the name of our first assessment of our patient?

131. What is a **"Scene Size-Up."**

132. What does *mnemonic* mean?

133. The mnemonic **PENMIRE** stands for what?

134. **GILT-D** stands for what?

135. **WIPEN** stands for what?

136. **AVPU** stands for what?

137. What type of painful stimulus are we allowed to use?

138. **A, B, C, D, E, F** and **TD**, stands for what?

139. What does **TIC** stand for?

140. What does **SAMPLE** stand for?

141. What is a **chief complaint**?

142. What does *Mechanism of Injury* mean?

143. List the standard *vital signs* we will obtain during our patient exam.

144. A *neurologic exam* will include what questions?

145. What does *OPQRST* stand for and for what condition are these questions most appropriate?

146. What does **AVPU** stand for?

147. What are the three **A/Ox3** questions?

148. *AEIOU-TIPS* is best used for what patient condition? What does it stand for?

Define these terms:

149. Contusion
150. Abrasion
151. Laceration
152. Crepitus
153. Asymmetry
154. Racoon eyes
155. Battles sign
156. Coffee ground emesis

157. Soot
158. Jugular veins
159. Carotid pulse
160. C-7
161. Accessory muscle
162. Tracheal deviation
163. Track marks
164. Subcutaneous emphysema
165. Stoma
166. Paradoxical chest movement
167. Sucking chest wound
168. Distention
169. Rigidity
170. Guarding
171. Masses
172. Priapism
173. Incontinence
174. Femoral pulse
175. Pedal pulse
176. Fistula
177. Renal
178. Sacral/sacrum

179. A "head-to-toe" exam may also be known as what?

180. What does *trauma naked* mean?

181. **DCAP-BLS** stands for what?

182. **ARDS** stands for what?

183. **MJ-CCATTS** stands for what?

184. **P-BASS** stands for what?

185. **DR-GMPS** stands for what?

186. **PPIB-F** stands for what?

187. **PMTS** stands for what?

188. **SST** stands for what?

189. What is the difference between BLS and ALS?

The Glasgow Coma Score *(Normal 4-5-6)*

190. What areas are assessed for each point?

Eye Opening
Stimuli needed for patient to open eyes
     4 =
     3 =
     2 =
     1 =

Verbal Response
Best communication when questioned
     5 =
     4 =
     3 =
     2 =
     1 =

Motor Response
Best response to command or stimulus
     6 =
     5 =
     4 =
     3 =
     2 =
     1 =

191. A perfect GCS is how many points?

192. The worst GCS score is how many points?

Other books by Lance Hodge

Available at **Amazon.com**, Booksamillion.com, Barnes & Noble, and other fine book sellers.

Including this:

The Common-Sense EMT: Thinking like an EMT made easy

By Lance Hodge
ISBN-13: 978-1672092715
$8.95
71 pages

Made in the USA
Las Vegas, NV
10 January 2023

65382132R00095